Internet safety

Intermediate 1
Course Handbook

✕ Ted Hastings ✕

Text © Ted Hastings
Design and layout © 2007 Leckie & Leckie
Cover image © Caleb Rutherford

01/031207

ISBN 978-1-84372-578-7

Published by
Leckie & Leckie Ltd, 3rd floor, 4 Queen Street, Edinburgh, EH2 1JE
Tel: 0131 220 6831 Fax: 0131 225 9987
enquiries@leckieandleckie.co.uk   www.leckieandleckie.co.uk

Special thanks to
Ellustration (design, page make-up and illustration), Roda Morrison (copyedit),
Ivor Normand (proofread), Caleb Rutherford (cover design).
A CIP Catalogue record for this book is available from the British Library.
® Leckie & Leckie is a registered trademark
Leckie & Leckie Ltd is a division of Huveaux plc.

Acknowledgements
Leckie & Leckie has made every effort to trace all copyright holders.
If any have been inadvertently overlooked, we will be pleased to make
the necessary arrangements.

Leckie & Leckie is grateful to the following for their permission
to reproduce material free of charge:
Team Spybot for a screenshot from Spybot (www.spybot.info),
Sunbelt Software for a screenshot from Counterspy (www.sunbelt-software.com),
Nationwide Building Society for use of a logo,
Steganos GmbH for a screenshot from Steganos (www.steganos.com),
Content Watch for a screenshot from Net Nanny (www.contentwatch.com),
Surf Control, Inc. for a screenshot from Cyberpatrol (www.cyberpatrol.com),
Net Applications for use of Market Share data (www.netapplications.com),
Microsoft product screenshots reprinted with permission from Microsoft Corporation.

CONTENTS

C

INTRODUCTION

In less than fifteen years, the Internet has fundamentally altered the world we live in. At the beginning of the 1990s, it was the province of a few academics and researchers and of little relevance to the rest of the world. Now it is used daily by adults from all walks of life for shopping, booking flights and holidays, communicating with family and friends and a myriad other purposes. It is also used by young people for playing games, sharing music and communicating with friends, as well as acting as a source of research information for school and college projects.

But the Internet can be a dangerous place. There are hackers out there who want to break into your system and steal or erase your data. There are companies who want to track your browsing and buying habits so they can advertise more effectively. There are people who want to steal your identity and the contents of your bank account, and predators who want to find and groom young victims. There are also people who want to use the Internet as a means of distributing pornography or hate-filled propaganda.

Fortunately, there are defences against all of these menaces. Antivirus and anti-spyware programs can prevent malware from being installed on your computer. Firewalls can deter hackers, and content-filtering software can block undesirable content. Regular back-ups can ensure that you can restore lost or corrupt data. And, perhaps most importantly, both adults and young people can learn to behave in ways that minimise or eliminate risks.

As long as you are prepared to take the right precautions, the Internet can be made safe. That is what this book is about. It explains what the dangers are, in simple and non-technical language, and tells you exactly what you need to do to combat them.

The book is designed to support the Internet Safety qualification offered by the Scottish Qualifications Authority, in schools and colleges across Scotland and further afield. This is thought to be the first Internet Safety qualification to be offered by a National Awarding body in the EU. It is delivered and assessed entirely online. This book will provide you with all the information you need to sit the online examination and will give suggestions for activities you can carry out to complete the practical requirements. All of the content is backed up by links to carefully selected Internet sites that will provide you with a wealth of further information.

However, even if you have no desire to obtain the qualification, the book still provides a comprehensive introduction to keeping yourself safe on the Internet.

The following links are to general Internet safety sites which will provide you with information on a variety of safety-related topics.

Be Safe Online: http://www.besafeonline.org/English/safer_use_of_services_on_the_internet.htm

Child Exploitation and Online Protection (CEOP) Centre: http://www.ceop.gov.uk/

Childnet: http://www.childnet-int.org/kia/

Get Safe Online: http://www.getsafeonline.org/

Netsafe: http://www.netsafe.smallmajority.co.uk/

Think U Know: http://www.thinkuknow.co.uk/

MALICIOUS SOFTWARE

- **Computer Viruses**
- **Types of Viruses**
- **Trojans and Worms**
- **Image Viruses**
- **Screensaver Viruses**
- **Antivirus Software**
- **Virus Hoaxes**
- **Major Virus Attacks**
- **Other Malicious Software**

COMPUTER VIRUSES

As soon as you connect a new computer to the Internet, it becomes vulnerable to attack from numerous types of **malicious software**, often shortened to **malware**. The US Government's Computer Emergency Response Team (CERT) estimates that new systems are often attacked within a few minutes of connection, unless steps are taken to protect them.

One of the commonest forms of attack is the **computer virus**. Almost everyone has heard of computer viruses, but very few people really understand them. After all, it seems strange that a virus can be passed between computers, in the same way as a virus like the common cold or measles can be passed between people.

What are they?

Computer viruses are small programs which make unauthorised modifications to the way a computer operates. Some are deliberately designed to damage your computer, for example by deleting or modifying files, or even by reformatting your hard disk. Others may only display a message or a welcome screen, but these are still a nuisance as they waste valuable resources. They can also contain errors or bugs that can cause computers to crash. The executable part of a computer virus is sometimes referred to as the **payload.**

All computer viruses have two essential features:

- They must be able to **execute** themselves. They will often attach themselves to another executable file, such as an application or utility program.
- They must be able to **replicate** or copy themselves. This is often done by replacing genuine programs with copies infected by the virus.

Computer viruses first appeared in the late 1980s, as usage of personal computers was beginning to grow. The first-ever virus is generally believed to be the **Morris Worm**, written by a student at Cornell University (USA) in 1988. By 1990, viruses had become a major problem, and they remain so today. Viruses were initially transferred between computers by means of infected floppy disks, but, as the use of computer networks, and later the Internet, rose, the scale of the threat increased dramatically.

Many virus attacks are directed at servers, particularly web servers, rather than end-user systems. These attacks are often designed to crash the system, or to make it run so slowly that it becomes useless to users. Attacks of this nature are known as **Denial of Service (DoS)** attacks. One famous technique which flooded systems with fake **ping** messages (normally used to check for the presence of a server) was known as the **ping of death**.

Viruses must be able to execute, and they must be able to replicate.

TYPES OF VIRUSES

Viruses can be classified in various ways, but it is generally agreed that there are five distinct types, all of which operate in different ways.

File Infector Viruses

As their name suggests, file infector viruses infect executable files or programs, such as games, utilities or applications. They are often **memory-resident**, meaning that once they are activated they remain lurking in memory, waiting to infect other programs. Viruses that do this are sometimes called 'resident viruses'. They can easily be transferred between computers via infected floppy disks, CD-ROMs or flash memory drives or transmitted over a network. Well-known file infector viruses include *Jerusalem* and *Cascade*.

Boot sector viruses

Boot sector viruses attach themselves to the **boot record** of a floppy disk or hard disk. The boot record is a small program that runs automatically when the computer is booted, or started up. If a computer is started from an infected disk, the virus will be transferred to memory and will infect any other disk which is inserted. Common boot sector viruses include *Michelangelo* and *Stoned*.

Master boot record viruses

These are similar to boot sector viruses, but they store an uninfected copy of the original boot record in another location. Many master boot record viruses are also **stealth viruses**, meaning that they try to hide themselves from antivirus software. Examples include *New York Boot (NYB)*, *AntiExe* and *Unashamed*.

Multipartite (or polypartite) viruses

Multipartite (or polypartite) viruses use a two-pronged attack which infects both boot records and executable files. They can be very difficult to get rid of, as both components must be removed. For example, if the boot sector is repaired, but infected files are left on the computer, the boot sector will simply be re-infected. Examples include *Emperor, Anthrax* and *Tequila*. Most viruses don't display much sign of their activities, but Tequila leaves an interesting image, as shown here:

```
Execute: mov ax, FE03 / int 21. Jey to go on

Welcome to T.TEQUILAs latest production.
Contact T.Tequila/P.O.Box 543/6312 St
hausen/Switzerland.
Loving thoughts to L.I.N.D.A

BEER and TEQUILA forever!
```

Macro viruses

Macro viruses infect data files. They take advantage of scripting languages or macro languages like VBA (Visual Basic for Applications), VBS (Visual Basic Script) or JavaScript. These are used to automate tasks in applications like Microsoft Office. Macro viruses are fairly easy to create and are now commonplace. Examples include *W97M.Melissa*, *WM.NiceDay* and *W97M.Groov*.

 This topic is assessed by means of multiple-choice questions, similar to those given at the end of this section.

 You can find out more about computer viruses at the following links:
Wikipedia: http://en.wikipedia.org/wiki/Computer_virus
How Stuff Works: http://www.howstuffworks.com/virus.htm
BBC Hot Topics: http://www.bbc.co.uk/science/hottopics/computerviruses/

TROJANS AND WORMS

Two other types of malware, **Trojans** and **Worms**, are very similar to viruses and are often mistakenly classed as viruses.

Trojans

A **Trojan** is a file which claims to do something useful but is actually malicious. The name comes from the Trojan Horse of Greek mythology, as seen in the film *Troy* (2004). Unlike viruses, Trojans do not replicate and they must be started by a user, for example by opening an **email attachment** or by downloading a file from the Internet. This is why you should never open email attachments unless you are certain of their source. Emails with attachments can often be recognised because they have a paperclip icon next to them in the list of messages. You should be very cautious when downloading programs. Trojans can cause loss or theft of data. *Trojan.Vundo* is one example.

Worms

Worms are malicious programs that replicate themselves from system to system without requiring human intervention, such as inserting a floppy or running a program. Worms are often hidden inside another file, such as a Word document or an Excel spreadsheet, but the whole document (rather than just the malicious code) travels from computer to computer and should be regarded as the worm. One example is *W32.Mydoom.AX@mm*, a mass-mailing worm that sends email to addresses it gathers from the Windows Address Book on a compromised computer. Some worms (e.g. *Blaster*) can allow a remote user to take control of your machine.

 Trojans do not replicate and must be started by a user. Worms can replicate without user action.

 You can find out more about Trojans and Worms at the following locations:
Wikipedia: Trojan Horse (Computing):
http://en.wikipedia.org/wiki/Trojan_horse_(computing)
Viruslist.com: Trojans:
http://www.viruslist.com/en/virusesdescribed?chapter=152540521
Wikipedia: Computer Worms: http://en.wikipedia.org/wiki/Computer_worm

IMAGE VIRUSES

One question that comes up frequently is whether or not computers can be infected by a virus contained within an image file. In September 2004, Microsoft published a patch for a major security flaw in the way many of its products dealt with the **JPEG graphics** format (.JPG). This flaw could allow attackers to create an image file that would run a malicious program on a victim's computer as soon as it was viewed. One of the vulnerable programs was Internet Explorer, so users could potentially be attacked simply by visiting a website that displayed infected images. Microsoft quickly released a tool to correct the flaw, and it was fixed permanently in Windows XP Service Pack 2.

Within a few weeks of Microsoft's announcement, a program that exploited the flaw had been posted to several newsgroups. The program was known as *Trojan.Moo* or *W32/Perrun*, but security experts did not regard it as a genuine virus, as it had no way of spreading and only threatened visitors to the relevant newsgroups who downloaded an image and viewed it in Internet Explorer. The program appeared to have been created by an automated tool known as the 'JPEG of Death' creation kit, and some experts expressed concern that this could be upgraded to produce a genuine virus threat.

Experts were also worried that antivirus programs would be unable to detect viruses embedded in JPEG files as they only scan executable files, but both Symantec and McAfee claim that their antivirus products can detect images containing malicious code.

SCREENSAVER VIRUSES

There have also been reports of viruses embedded in **screensaver** files. These have the file extension .SCR. In July 2007, it was reported that users worldwide had received emails claiming that the recipient had been sent a screensaver by a friend and telling the user to open the attachment **bsaver.zip**. When opened, this file infected PCs with the *Troj/Agent-FZB Trojan*, which dropped two rootkits.

There have been numerous reports of a **Budweiser Frogs** screensaver containing a virus, but these have all turned out to be hoaxes.

ANTIVIRUS SOFTWARE

Antivirus software is used to prevent viruses (and sometimes other forms of malware) from infecting a computer system or to remove them after it has been infected. Antivirus software is available from a number of companies. The best-known one is probably Norton. At the time of writing, the latest version is **Norton Antivirus 2008**, which includes antivirus, Internet worm protection, anti-spyware and rootkit detection.

According to the company's website, the product has the following features:

- Detects and removes spyware and viruses.
- Blocks spyware and worms automatically.
- Prevents virus-infected emails from spreading.
- Rootkit detection finds and removes hidden threats.

McAfee is another major supplier of antivirus software. Their current product is **Virus Scan Plus**, which offers protection from viruses, hackers and spyware by integrating antivirus, firewall and anti-spyware technologies. It also warns users about sites which send spam, install adware or attempt online scams.

According to the company's website, the product has the following features:

- Stops viruses. Automatically blocks, cleans and removes viruses so you can surf the web safely and download files.
- Blocks spyware. Blocks spyware before it installs on your computer and removes existing spyware so you can surf the web safely.
- Stops hackers. Protects and conceals your computer from hackers so you can surf the Internet safely.

Another interesting product is **AVG Antivirus,** which is free to home and non-commercial users and provides a high level of detection capability.

According to the company's website, the product has the following features:
- Easy to use, low system resources
- Automatic update functionality
- Real-time protection as files are opened and programs are run
- AVG's Virus Vault for the safe handling of infected files.

There are many other suppliers of antivirus software, including Panda, Steganos,

Trend Micro, Kaspersky and Bullguard. You can find links to their websites at the foot of this section. Almost all of them allow you to download time-limited demo versions of their software, since antivirus software producers make most of their money from subscriptions to update services rather than from the sale of the software itself.

Some suppliers, including Trend Micro, Kaspersky and Panda, offer free online scans which will check your system for viruses. Unfortunately, these tools will not remove viruses, so if any are found you will be invited to buy the full product to remove them.

How does antivirus software work?

Antivirus software normally relies on two techniques: checking files for known viruses matching definitions in a virus dictionary, and watching for suspicious behaviour from any computer program which might indicate an attack. Most commercial antivirus software uses a combination of these approaches and relies on frequent updates to the virus dictionary as new viruses are discovered.

Dictionary-based antivirus software generally checks files each time they are opened, closed or emailed, so that it can detect viruses as soon as they are received. It can also be configured to scan the system at regular intervals, e.g. in the middle of the night when no-one will be using it. The dictionary approach is generally successful, but some virus writers have tried to defeat it by producing **polymorphic viruses**, which change themselves so that they no longer match the recorded signatures.

The **behavioural** approach monitors the behaviour of all programs, looking for suspicious activities such as attempting to modify an executable file, and warning users if it encounters anything unusual. This approach gives some protection against new viruses, but unfortunately it generates a large number of false alarms.

Another recent approach is **whitelisting** the programs that are allowed to run, rather than blocking those which are not. If a program is not on the whitelist, it isn't permitted to run.

One advantage of this approach is that it blocks all unwanted programs, not just viruses and malware. However, it can be difficult to ensure that whitelists are kept up to date with all permitted software, particularly in large organisations.

Norton: http://www.symantec.com/en/uk/norton/products/overview.jsp?pcid=is&pvid=nav2008

McAfee: http://www.mcafee-downloads.co.uk/virus-scan-plus.htm

AVG Free: http://free.grisoft.com/doc/2/

Panda: http://www.pandasoftware.co.uk/2007/02210-PandaAntivirus.htm

Steganos: https://www.steganos.com/uk/products/home-office/antivirus/overview/

Trend Micro: http://uk.trendmicro.com/uk/products/personal/antivirus-plus-anti-spyware/index.html

Kaspersky: http://www.kaspersky.co.uk/

Bullguard: http://www.bullguard.com/

VIRUS HOAXES

As if there wasn't enough of a problem with real viruses, there are also lots of virus hoaxes about. These are usually email messages which use pseudo-technical language and claim to warn users of a dangerous new virus, quoting an authority such as Microsoft or CNN. They often ask users to forward a copy to all their contacts, leading to vast amounts of wasted time. Some hoaxes are more malicious, as they ask users to delete little-known system files which can prevent a computer from running properly. If you receive an email that warns you of a virus and asks you to forward it to your contacts, the best bet is to ignore it and delete it. If you are curious, you can check if it is genuine at the websites listed in Internet Links below.

One recent hoax was the Olympic Torch warning shown below:

Please read the attached warning issued today.

PLEASE FORWARD THIS WARNING AMONG FRIENDS, FAMILY AND CONTACTS:

You should be alert during the next days:

Do not open any message with an attached file called "Invitation" regardless of who sent it .

It is a virus that opens an Olympic Torch which "burns" the whole hard disc C of your computer. This virus will be received from someone who has your e-mail address in his/her contact list, that is why you should send this e-mail to all your contacts. It is better to receive this message 25 times than to receive the virus and open it.

If you receive a mail called "invitation", though sent by a friend, do not open it and shut down your computer immediately.

This is the worst virus announced by CNN, it has been classified by Microsoft as the most destructive virus ever.

This virus was discovered by McAfee yesterday, and there is no repair yet for this kind of virus.

This virus simply destroys the Zero Sector of the Hard Disc, where the vital information is kept.

SEND THIS E-MAIL TO EVERYONE YOU KNOW, COPY THIS E-MAIL AND SEND IT TO YOUR FRIENDS AND REMEMBER: IF YOU SEND IT TO THEM, YOU WILL BENEFIT ALL OF US.

Never pass on a virus hoax e-mail to your friends. Delete it and forget it!

You can find out more about virus hoaxes at the following locations:
Hoaxbusters: http://hoaxbusters.ciac.org/
Symantec: http://www.symantec.com/enterprise/security_response/threatexplorer/risks/hoaxes.jsp

MAJOR VIRUS ATTACKS

Blaster (2003)

The *Blaster* worm, also known as *Lovsan* or *MSBlast*, exploited a weakness in Windows 2000/XP and was transmitted over the Internet and Local Area Networks. When activated, it displayed a dialog box stating that the system was about to shut down. The virus contained hidden messages, including one addressed to Bill Gates. It also contained code to carry out a DoS attack on Microsoft's Windows Update site, but fortunately it had largely been eliminated before the trigger date arrived.

Sobig.F (2003)

Sobig.F infected over a million host computers in 24 hours via innocent-looking e-mail attachments. It transmitted itself to email addresses found on infected machines, swamping the Internet with vast amounts of traffic. The virus deactivated itself on 10 September 2003. Microsoft has offered a quarter-million dollar reward for the author, but no-one has yet been caught.

Bagle (2004)

The *Bagle* worm infected systems via an email attachment and then searched for email addresses it could replicate itself to. Some of its variants also opened a back door which allowed remote users to access confidential information on an infected system.

The original version of *Bagle* stopped spreading at the end of January 2004, but some variants are still current and continue to cause problems.

MyDoom (2004)

MyDoom, also known as *Norvarg*, was a mass mailing worm, distributed as an email attachment. The attachment name, subject and content were chosen randomly by the worm. If the attachment was opened, the virus transmitted itself to all the email addresses found on the infected machine. It also used email addresses collected by search engines and could be transmitted via Kazaa peer-to-peer networking accounts. At its peak, *MyDoom* slowed global Internet performance by up to 50 per cent and it has been estimated that in the first few hours after its appearance up to 10 per cent of all e-mail messages were infected.

In the online exam, you could be asked questions about viruses, Trojans and worms. These will be in a similar form to the Test Yourself questions given at the end of this chapter. Try to remember what the viruses shown in this section look like. You may be asked to recognise them from pictures in the online exam.

Now would be a good time to complete the section of your log book dealing with viruses. In addition to giving a brief summary of what you've learned about viruses, and how to avoid and combat them, either you should describe your experiences in installing and configuring antivirus software or you should compare the different antivirus solutions available. Your tutor should be able to advise you as to which task you should complete.

OTHER MALICIOUS SOFTWARE

Spyware

Spyware, as the name suggests, is software that can monitor a user's activities on a computer or even take partial control of the computer. It is almost always installed without the user's consent and is often used to collect personal information (including financial information such as credit card numbers) and transmit it to some external destination.

Spyware can also install additional software on computers and 'hijack' web browsers, redirecting them to pages other than those requested by the user, usually advertising sites, or sites which will download more spyware. Other functions can include delivering pop-up advertising and monitoring of websites visited.

Spyware normally hides itself from the user, displaying no visible icons in the taskbar or obvious signs that the program is active. Spyware programs do not normally provide an uninstall routine. This is different from legitimate software, which will always provide an easy method of uninstalling the application.
It is difficult to find out just how many computers are infected by spyware, but recent surveys have suggested that it could range between 60 per cent and 90 per cent of PCs, with the vast majority of users being unaware that their PCs are infected.

Sources of spyware

Spyware does not spread in the same way as viruses or worms, and infected systems do not usually try to pass on the infection to others. One common source of spyware infections is **peer-to-peer** (P2P) file-sharing programs, including well-known ones like **Kazaa** and **Limewire**. Spyware is often bundled with these, in a similar manner to a Trojan, and installed surreptitiously when the user installs the program. In some instances, the file-sharing program will stop working if the spyware is removed.

Spyware has also been found in other supposedly useful utility programs, such as web-accelerators, and worms or viruses have occasionally been found to deliver a spyware payload. Another route of infection is to trick the user into visiting a website which invisibly downloads and installs the software. This is sometimes referred to as a **'drive-by' download**.

Internet security companies have recently reported a massive increase in websites of this nature. Drive-by downloads can be minimised by ensuring that your browser software is up to date and by making the security setting high enough to detect unauthorised downloads, e.g. at least the 'Medium' setting for Internet Explorer.

Effects of spyware

Spyware infections can seriously degrade the performance of a system by causing increased processor usage, disk activity or network traffic, all of which can slow the system down. Spyware can often cause applications or systems to crash and may make connecting to the Internet difficult. Users often fail to realise that spyware is the culprit and look first for hardware or software problems, or even viruses.

Spyware infections seldom come alone. Once a computer has been infected initially, it will often become subject to multiple infections, leading to a dramatic deterioration in performance. In the worst cases, it may be necessary to wipe the hard disk completely and reinstall the operating system and applications in order to cleanse a machine of spyware.

 You can read a real-life example of one teenager's experiences with spyware here: http://www.download.com/Spyware-Horror-Stories/1200-2023_4-5178025.html

Spyware clues

According to the US Federal Trade Commission (FTC), the following may be clues that you have spyware on your system:

- a barrage of pop-up ads
- a hijacked browser – that is, a browser that takes you to sites other than those you type into the address box
- a sudden or repeated change in your computer's Internet home page
- new and unexpected toolbars
- new and unexpected icons on the system tray at the bottom of your computer screen
- keys that don't work (for example, the 'Tab' key that might not work when you try to move to the next field in a web form)
- random error messages
- sluggish or downright slow performance when opening programs or saving files.

The FTC suggests that the following steps can help you avoid spyware:

- Update your operating system and web-browser software.
- Download free software only from sites you know and trust.
- Don't install any software without knowing exactly what it is.
- Minimise 'drive-by' downloads.
- Don't click on any links within pop-up windows.
- Don't click on links in spam that claim to offer anti-spyware software.
- Install a personal firewall to stop uninvited users from accessing your computer.

Spyware examples

Spyware programs can be classified in many different ways. The names given to them by vendors of anti-spyware software may not be the same as those given by their creators. Spyware programs are often classed together by common behaviour rather than because of similarities in their code. Spyware programs which come from the same source may be classified together although they operate in different ways.

- **CoolWebSearch** is a group of programs which takes advantage of browser vulnerabilities to direct traffic to advertising websites such as *coolwebsearchcom.* It also displays pop-up advertisements, changes search engine results, and alters the infected computer's files to misdirect searches. It is notoriously difficult to detect and remove, as so many different versions exist.

■ **Brilliant Digital Entertainment (BDE)** not only monitors Internet use on infected computers, it also uses them to store and serve advertisements and to process data collected from other users. It is extremely widespread because it was bundled (under the name of *BDE Projector*) with many versions of the Kazaa file-sharing program. The suppliers of Kazaa claim that no spyware is bundled with the current version of the program, but some experts believe that this is simply because the spyware functions have now been incorporated into the main program.

■ **Hotbar** adds graphical skins (photographic overlays) to the Internet Explorer, Outlook and Outlook Express toolbars and also adds its own toolbar (shown below) and search button. The toolbars have keyword-targeted advertisements built into them. Hotbar can transmit details of the websites visited by users to various servers, which may be used for marketing purposes.

 You can find lots of additional information about Hotbar at:
http://ca.com/us/securityadvisor/pest/pest.aspx?id=453075474

Spyware and the law

The **Computer Misuse Act 1990** makes unauthorised access to a computer a criminal offence in the UK. Similar laws apply in other countries. This suggests that the activities of spyware authors and distributors are illegal, as they lead to unauthorised installation of software. If the spyware writers collect personal information, then the use they make of it may be subject to the provisions of the **Data Protection Act 1998.**

However, things are seldom as simple as this. Many of the programs that install spyware ask the user to accept an **End User Licence Agreement (EULA)** which is so broad that it gives the software supplier permission to do practically anything. These EULAs often use complex legal language which makes them difficult for the average user to understand, so many users simply go ahead and click to accept the EULA without really reading it.

No fewer than three different federal acts to curb spyware are currently being considered in the USA: the **Internet Spyware Prevention Act (I-SPY Act)**, the **Securely Protect Yourself Against Cyber Trespass Act (SPY Act)** and the **Software Principles Yielding Better Levels of Computer Knowledge Act (SPY BLOCK Act)**. These bills are designed to criminalise the unauthorised installation of software, impose a requirement to disclose information to users, and protect users from surreptitious transmission of personal information. There will probably be some consolidation of these bills before they become law.

You can find a useful summary of the legal issues relating to spyware, in both the UK and the USA, at:
http://news.zdnet.co.uk/itmanagement/0,1000000308,39172719-1,00.htm

Anti-spyware software

Many software suppliers have now released programs designed to remove or intercept spyware, one of the earliest being **Spybot – Search & Destroy** from Safer Networking. Another popular program was **Giant Anti-Spyware,** which was bought over by Microsoft before being upgraded and renamed as **Microsoft Defender**.

Grisoft, vendors of the popular **AVG Anti-Virus** program, acquired anti-spyware firm Ewido Networks and re-released their anti-spyware program as **AVG Anti-Spyware**. Like AVG Anti-Virus, AVG Anti-Spyware is available in a

free version for home users. Other well-known anti-spyware software includes **Anti-Spyware** from Trend Micro, **Spyware Doctor** from PC Tools and **CounterSpy** from Sunbelt Software.

Major antivirus firms such as **Symantec**, **McAfee** and **Sophos** have also added anti-spyware features to their security suites.

How anti-spyware software works
Anti-spyware programs carry out two distinct tasks:
- **Detection and removal of spyware:** users can schedule daily, weekly or monthly scans to detect and remove any spyware that has been installed. The software scans the contents of the Windows registry, operating system files and installed programs and generates a list of any threats detected, allowing users to choose whether to keep or delete files.
- **Real-time protection against incoming spyware:** this operates in a similar manner to antivirus software. It can prevent spyware from entering your system and being installed. This is generally done by comparing the characteristics of downloads against those of known spyware programs.

Many anti-spyware programs rely on a **database** of threats. Since new threats appear daily, most spyware programs are of little use unless this database is updated regularly. Many programs carry out database updates automatically.

Spyware is notoriously difficult to uninstall. Some programs work by having two processes running simultaneously. If one process is killed off, the other promptly restarts it. This can sometimes be overcome by killing off the entire process tree (a group of related processes) or by carrying out the removal in **Safe Mode**, a special diagnostic mode of Windows which can be selected at start-up. Other programs detect any attempt to delete registry keys and immediately restore them. Some recent spyware programs (e.g. **Look2Me**) can detect the existence of anti-spyware software and stop it from running correctly.

Fake anti-spyware programs

One of the biggest spyware problems is the ever-increasing number of fake anti-spyware programs around. These programs (often referred to as rogue software) claim to help remove spyware from your computer, but often do nothing and may even install spyware. They often display banner advertisements telling users that their computer has been infected and urging them to download or buy a program to remove the infection. Examples include **Spyware Quake**, **Spy Sheriff** and **Spyware Cleaner**.

The writers of rogue software don't lack imagination when it comes to distributing their product. Recently, there has been a spate of pop-ups encouraging users to download 'anti-spyware' programs appearing in user profiles on **YouTube**, where many users are fairly naïve regarding security.

 You can find out more about rogue software links on YouTube at:
http://blog.spywareguide.com/2007/06/rogue_security_applications_be.html

Other anti-spyware precautions

Most spyware attacks are directed against Microsoft's **Internet Explorer** web browser, both because it has the largest installed user base (around 60 per cent of the market) and because it is fairly lax about downloading and running potentially harmful programs, although users can restrict this feature. One way of avoiding spyware is to use an alternative browser, such as Opera or Firefox, although this does not guarantee security, and attacks against Firefox (which has around 33 per cent of the market) are on the increase.

Some ISPs use firewalls or proxy servers (these are discussed in greater detail later) to block websites which are known sources of spyware.

Shareware programs can be a major source of spyware, so it's always best to download them from a reputable site, such as Download.com, which checks all downloadable files for spyware before making them available.

 You can download the Opera web browser from: http://www.opera.com/
You can download the Firefox web browser from:
http://www.mozilla-europe.org/en/products/firefox/

Adware

Adware is the name given to any software that displays advertisements. Adware is generally regarded as a type of spyware because it selects the advertisements to be displayed on the basis of the user's browsing habits. Examples include Gator and BargainBuddy, which are often installed as drive-by downloads without the knowledge of the user. Most users object to pop-up ads. At best, they can be visually annoying, but in some cases they can be offensive or even illegal, e.g. where pop-ups advertising adult sites or gambling sites can be viewed by children.

Many anti-spyware and anti-adware programs also act as pop-up blockers. Although some pop-ups are legitimate, many of them are adware, and some can even be a source of further spyware or adware attacks. Modern web browsers such as Internet Explorer 7 or Firefox 3.0 also have pop-up-blocking features.

Some shareware programs, such as the Eudora email client, display advertisements rather than charging registration fees. Software of this nature is probably better described as 'advertising-supported software'. It is normally installed with the knowledge of the user and may even provide a useful service.

Adware has even started appearing on MySpace. A well-known adware company called Zango has been creating profiles with video links in them. If you click on one of these, a pop-up launches, as shown below, inviting you to accept a licence to play a video file. If you do, you'll be installing the Zango Search Assistant and Toolbar.

In November 2006, Zango was fined by the Federal Trade Commission (FTC), as can be seen by the following quote from the FTC's website:

'Zango, Inc., formerly known as 180solutions, Inc., one of the world's largest distributors of adware, and two principals have agreed to settle Federal Trade Commission charges that they used unfair and deceptive methods to download adware and obstruct consumers from removing it, in violation of federal law. The settlement bars future downloads of Zango's adware without consumers' consent, requires Zango to provide a way for consumers to remove the adware, and requires them to give up $3 million in ill-gotten gains.'

 Spyware and adware can cause a serious deterioration in the performance of your computer and can also lead to the loss of confidential data. You should always ensure that you are protected against them by installing suitable anti-spyware software.

 You can read about Zango's attempts to distribute adware via MySpace here: http://www.vitalsecurity.org/2006/07/teenagers-used-to-push-zango-on.html
You can read the FTC report on Zango here:
http://www.ftc.gov/opa/2006/11/zango.shtm

Rogue diallers

Rogue diallers are programs which take over a user's modem, causing it to dial out to a premium-rate number and possibly rack up a huge telephone bill. They can take control while a user is actually surfing, dropping the current connection and reconnecting via the premium-rate number. They have also been known to activate themselves if a user leaves a machine unattended for a period of time.

Rogue diallers are generally only considered to be a problem for dial-up users – they do not affect broadband users. However, broadband users who have a dial-up modem installed should be careful to ensure that it is disconnected from the telephone line, otherwise there is still a possibility of a rogue dialler taking charge.

Most rogue diallers are downloaded via drive-by downloads, without the user being aware that this has happened. However, they can also infect systems via email, particularly by users of Outlook Express, which allows emails containing embedded code to be previewed, releasing the rogue dialler into the system. Rogue diallers can run up enormous bills, sometimes as much as £2 000.

Telephone companies have been reluctant to accept responsibility for the cost incurred by rogue diallers, maintaining that it is the responsibility of users to ensure that their computers are kept free of malware. BT supplies a software utility that warns users if their modem is being used to call a premium-rate or international number.

Rogue diallers have been investigated by the Federal Trade Commission in the USA and by the Office of Fair Trading in the UK; and ICSTIS, the UK watchdog for premium-rate phone services, has already shut down a number of premium-rate services. However, service operators often respond by moving their operations overseas to countries with fewer controls in place.

 You can get more information about rogue diallers at:
http://www.bbc.co.uk/webwise/askbruce/articles/security/roguediallers_1.shtml

Unsecured wireless connections

The recent expansion in the use of wireless (WiFi) networks in both home and business settings has led to a growth in the number of attacks on wireless systems. There are two distinct types of attacks: passive and active.

Passive attacks are difficult to detect because the attackers never join your network; they simply capture data, which could include confidential personal information, for later analysis. Attackers may be able to capture account details and passwords, for email accounts or bank accounts, allowing them later access to these accounts from any computer. They may also be able to build up a record of your web-browsing activities.

Active attacks can potentially do more damage than passive attacks. For example, if you have shared files on your PC, then attackers may be able to access or even change data on your hard disk via an unsecured wireless network. An unsecured link may allow attackers access to the entire network. Attackers have also been known to launch spam or virus attacks via systems that they have hacked into from an unsecured wireless network.

Fortunately, these problems can be avoided by ensuring that your wireless network is properly secured. However, wireless network security is a complex topic, and the steps involved can vary depending on the operating system that you are running and the wireless router you are using. The best idea is to seek the advice of your ISP. They should be able to tell you how to configure your network and router for maximum security. This information may be available in the manual they issue to users, or on their website.

A slightly different problem can arise if you are connecting to a wireless network via a public or private **hotspot.** You have no control over how the hotspot providers are monitoring network traffic, and you don't know how good their protection against intruders is. The best advice that can be given here is to try to avoid sending any type of confidential data when you are logged into a public hotspot.

 Unsecured wireless networks can leave you open to attack. If you are running a wireless network, make sure it is secured as recommended by your ISP.

 You can read more about Wireless Network Security at: http://compnetworking.about com/od/wirelesssecurity/tp/wifisecurity.htm

Key loggers

A **key logger** is a program which monitors and logs every key a user presses. More sophisticated versions log everything a user does: keystrokes, mouse clicks, files opened and closed, sites visited etc. Some programs can also capture text from windows or record everything displayed on the screen, e.g. the contents of files opened by the user. Key loggers can be used to capture passwords, credit card numbers and other information a user may not wish to reveal. The information captured can be stored locally or transmitted to an external system.

Key loggers are sometimes used by employers to monitor the activities of their staff, but they are more commonly encountered as a type of spyware. They are often included in rootkits (see page 38).

Key loggers can be made up of multiple files and are normally hidden completely

 If you want to see how a key logger works, you can download a trial version of Actual Spy from: http://www.actualspy.com/download.html. This will allow you to monitor keyboard activity for forty minutes and view the results.

 You can download a free trial copy of Anti-Keylogger from: http://www.anti-keyloggers.com/
In the online exam, you could be asked questions about spyware, adware, rogue diallers and key loggers. These will be in a similar form to the Test Yourself questions given at the end of this chapter.

 Now would be a good time to complete the section of your log book dealing with spyware. In addition to giving a brief summary of what you've learned about spyware, and how to avoid and combat it, either you should describe your experiences in installing and configuring anti-spyware software or you should compare the different anti-spyware solutions available. Your tutor should be able to advise you as to which task you should complete.
You should be able to find plenty of information about the different solutions available by using a search engine such as Google.

from the user. This makes them difficult to detect and remove manually, since if one file is deleted the others can restore it. Unsuccessful or incomplete removal attempts can result in system instability or crashes. Fortunately, most major anti-spyware programs can detect and remove key loggers. There are also a number of specialist anti-keylogging programs available, such as **Anti-Keylogger**.

Ransomware

Ransomware is a type of malware that encrypts the data on a computer and demands a ransom to restore it. The earliest example of this type of malware was the **PC Cyborg Trojan** (1989), which encrypted filenames, causing the file system to be corrupted. Other ransomware attacks have included **Ransom-A**, which threatened to delete a file every thirty minutes unless victims paid $10.99, and **Arhiveus-A**, which asked victims to buy pills from an online drug store rather than asking for money.

Ransomware attacks appear to have been on the increase since the middle of 2005. Examples include **Gpcode**, **TROJ.RANSOM.A**, **Archiveus**, **Krotten**, **Cryzip** and **MayArchive**. **Gpcode-AI** encrypts data on infected machines then demands money from users to decrypt it. It also includes backdoor key-logging features. Gpcode-AI encrypts every document on the hard disk and creates a file called *read_me.txt* containing the scammers' demands:

```
Hello, your files are encrypted with RSA-4096 algorithm (http://
en.wikipedia.org/wiki/RSA).

You will need at least few years to decrypt these files without
our software. All your private information for last 3 months were
collected and sent to us.

To decrypt your files you need to buy our software. The price is $300.
To buy our software please contact us at: xxxxxxx@xxxxx.com and
provide us your personal code -xxxxxxxxx. After successful purchase we
will send your decrypting tool, and your private information will be
deleted from our system.

If you will not contact us until 07/15/2007 your private information
will be shared and you will lose all your data.
```

The scammers claim that payment must be made by a given deadline or data will be unrecoverable, but this is simply a trick to encourage users to pay up rapidly, as the code is not capable of deleting the encrypted data.

Antivirus software producers have released updates to combat Gpcode-AI, but they warn that the encryption techniques being used for ransomware are becoming more complex and that they may soon become too difficult to decrypt in a reasonable amount of time without access to the encryption key generated by the scammers.

The surest way to guard against ransomware is to take regular back-ups of your data so that, in the unfortunate event of it being encrypted, it can be restored from back-up.

> You can read the details of a real-life ransomware attack at:
> http://news.bbc.co.uk/2/hi/uk_news/england/manchester/5034384.stm

Spam

Spamming is the abuse of electronic messaging systems, particularly email, to send unsolicited bulk messages. Messages must be both unsolicited and bulk to be classed as spam, as there are legitimate uses for both unsolicited email (e.g. initial contacts or enquiries) and bulk email (e.g. opt-in mailing lists). It has been estimated that up to 90 per cent of all emails are spam.

The term 'spam' is a reference to a sketch broadcast on the 1970s TV comedy show *Monty Python's Flying Circus*. The sketch takes place in a café where almost every item on the menu includes Spam. You can easily find a video of the original sketch by searching for 'Monty Python Spam' on YouTube.

Spammers can obtain email addresses from a variety of sources, including addresses published on websites and newsgroups. They also use **dictionary attacks**, programs which try to generate every possible email address for a particular server. This is why you can find yourself receiving spam, even when you've tried to keep your email address secret. Spammers also sell one another mailing lists with millions of email addresses.

One particular version of spam is known as a **mail bomb**. This involves sending thousands or even millions of spam messages to a single email address with the intention of clogging up, or even crashing, mail servers and mailboxes. This is a form of **DoS (Denial of Service)** attack.

Spam advertising

Most spam messages contain advertising, often for online pharmacies, gambling, pornography or bogus share dealings. Unfortunately, spam is a cheap means of advertising, as the only cost involved is building a mailing list. The costs of dealing with spam, mostly in terms of wasted time and bandwidth, fall upon ISPs, employers and individual users. These costs have been estimated at around $200 billion (£100 billion) per year. Spammers often receive a commission, sometimes as high as 50 per cent, if the recipient buys something. The potential rewards can be huge – some spammers have claimed to make as much as $10 000 to $15 000 per week.

Spam in other media

Although email spam is the commonest, spam is also found in other media, including instant messaging systems, text messages, blogs, wikis and e-groups. Spam has also started appearing on online video sites such as YouTube. Spammers copy a commercial and re-post it on **YouTube**, or add it as a comment to another video. A related problem is **Instant Messaging spam**, sometimes referred to as **spim**, which targets instant messaging systems, such as Windows Live Messenger or Yahoo Messenger. **Mobile phone spam** (spaSMS) using text messages is also on the increase. This can be particularly annoying to users, such as those travelling abroad, who are charged for receiving text messages.

The 'Spam King'

It can be difficult for the law to catch up with spammers, but it does happen occasionally. In May 2007, Robert Alan Soloway, known as the 'Spam King' and believed to be one of the world's top ten spammers, was arrested in Washington on charges including mail fraud, wire fraud, email fraud, identity theft and money laundering. He could receive a sentence of up to twenty years in prison if convicted.

Soloway is said to have made more than $750 000 by using 'zombie' computers to send out millions of spam emails since 2003. ('Zombies' are computers infected by a Trojan which allows an intruder to post spam from them without the knowledge of the owner.) He offered clients software which would allow them to send out spam emails to more than 80 million addresses. Unfortunately, his arrest does not appear to have led to any major reduction in the amount of spam in circulation.

The Nigerian Letter scam

Spam has also been used for sending political or religious messages, distributing viruses and attempting fraud. One of the most famous spam messages is a type of advance-fee fraud, known as the **Nigerian Letter**. Victims receive email from Nigeria, or another overseas country, asking for help in transferring large sums of money out of the country. They are asked to provide details of a bank account that can be used to transfer the money, and are offered a percentage in exchange.

Just before the transaction is due to take place, they are informed that they need to pay a few thousand dollars to cover administration charges. Anyone foolish enough to be taken in by this scam finds that the administration charges vanish and the mythical large sums of money never appear.

A typical letter is shown below. Many Nigerian Letter fraudsters appear to use keyboards that only have uppercase characters!

DR. IKE ODUMA
LAGOS, NIGERIA.
ATTENTION: PRESIDENT/CEO.
Please respond by fax to United Kingdom Private efax:
44 870 831 7247

DEAR SIR,

REQUEST FOR URGENT BUSINESS RELATIONSHIP.
FIRSTLY I MUST SOLICIT YOUR STRICTEST CONFIDENCE IN
THIS SUBJECT. THIS IS BY VIRTUE OF IT_S NATURE AS
BEING UTTERLY CONFIDENTIAL AND TOP SECRET. A MEMBER
OF THE NIGERIA EXPORT PROMOTION COUNCIL (N.E.P.C.)
WHO WAS PART OF THE FEDERAL GOVERNMENT DELEGATION
TO YOUR COUNTRY DURING A TRADE EXHIBITION GAVE
YOUR PARTICULARS TO ME. I HAVE DECIDED TO SEEK A
CONFIDENTIAL OPERATION WITH YOU IN THE EXECUTION OF
THE DEAL DESCRIBED HEREUNDER FOR THE BENEFIT OF ALL
THE PARTIES AND HOPE THAT YOU KEEP IT TOP SECRET
BECAUSE OF THE NATURE OF THE BUSINESS.

WITHIN THE MINISTRY OF PETROLEUM RESOURCES WHERE
I WORK AS A DIRECTOR OF ENGINEERING AND PROJECTS,
AND WITH THE CO-OPERATION OF FOUR OTHER VERY TOP
OFFICIALS, WE HAVE UNDER OUR CONTROL AS OVERDUE
CONTRACT PAYMENTS, BILLS TOTALING THIRTY ONE MILLION
UNITED STATES DOLLARS, WHICH WE WANT TO TRANSFER TO A
FOREIGN ACCOUNT, WITH THE ASSISTANCE AND CO-OPERATION
OF A FOREIGN COMPANY TO RECEIVE THE SAID FUNDS ON OUR
BEHALF OR A RELIABLE FOREIGN INDIVIDUAL ACCOUNT TO
RECEIVE THE FUNDS.

THE SOURCE OF THE FUND IS AS FOLLOWS: DURING THE LAST
MILITARY GOVERNMENT HERE IN NIGERIA WHICH LASTED BOUT
ELEVEN MONTHS, GOVERNMENT OFFICIALS SET UP COMPANIES
AND AWARDED THEMSELVES VARIOUS CONTRACTS WHICH WERE
GROSSLY OVER-INVOICED IN VARIOUS MINISTRIES. THE
PRESENT CIVILIAN GOVERNMENT IS NOT AWARE OF THE
ATROCITIES COMMITTED BY THEIR PREDECESSORS AND AS A
RESULT, WE HAVE A LOT OF SUCH OVER INVOICED CONTRACT
PAYMENT S PENDING WHICH WE HAVE IDENTIFIED FLOATING
AT THE CENTRAL BANK OF NIGERIA READY FOR PAYMENT.
HOWEVER BY VIRTUE OF OUR POSITION AS CIVIL SERVANTS,
WE CANNOT ACQUIRE THIS MONEY IN OUR NAMES. I WAS
THEREFORE DELEGATED AS A MATTER OF URGENCY BY MY

COLLEAGUES TO LOOK FOR AN OVER SEAS PARTNER INTO WHOSE ACCOUNT WE WOULD TRANSFER THE SUM OF   US$31,000,000.00 (THIRTY ONE MILLION UNITED STATES DOLLARS) HENCE WE ARE WRITING YOU THIS LETTER.

SINCE THE PRESENT CIVILIAN GOVERNMENT IS DETERMINED TO PAY FOREIGN CONTRACTORS L DEBTS OWED SO AS TO MAINTAIN AN AMIABLE RELATIONSHIP WITH FOREIGN GOVERNMENTS AND NON GOVERNMENT FINANCIAL AGENCIES. WE HAVE DECIDED TO INCLUDE OUR BILLS FOR APPROVAL WITH THE CO-OPERATION OF SOME OFFICIALS OF THE FEDERAL MINISTRY OF FINANCE (F.M.F) AND THE CENTRAL BANK OF NIGERIA (C.B.N). WE ARE SEEKING YOUR ASSISTANCE IN PROVIDING US WITH A GOOD COMPANY ACCOUNT OR ANY OTHER OFFSHORE BANK ACCOUNT INTO WHICH WE CAN REMIT THIS MONEY BY ACTING OUR MAIN PARTNER AND TRUSTEE OR ACTING AS THE ORIGINAL CONTRACTOR. THIS WE CAN DO BY SWAPPING OF ACCOUNT INFORMATION AND CHANGING OF BENEFICIARY AND OTHER PERTINENT INFORMATION TO APPLY FOR PAYMENT. BY THIS ACT, WE WOULD BE USING YOUR COMPANY INFORMATION TO APPLY FOR PAYMENT, AND PREPARE LETTERS OF CLAIM AND JOB DESCRIPTION ON BEHALF OF YOUR COMPANY. THIS PROCESS WOULD BE AN INTERNAL ARRANGEMENT WITH THE DEPARTMENTS CONCERNED.

I HAVE THE AUTHORITY OF MY PARTNERS INVOLVED TO PROPOSE THAT SHOULD YOU BE WILLING TO ASSIST US IN THIS TRANSACTION, YOUR SHARE AS COMPENSATION WILL BE US$6.2 MILLION (20%), US$21.7 MILLION (70%) FOR US AND US$3.1 (10%) FOR TAXATION AND MISCELLANEOUS EXPENSES.

THE BUSINESS ITSELF IS 100% SAFE, PROVIDED YOU TREAT IT WITH UTMOST SECRECY AND CONFIDENTIALITY. ALSO YOUR RE OF SPECIALIZATION IS NOT M HINDRANCE TO THE SUCCESSFUL EXECUTION OF THIS TRANSACTION. I HAVE REPOSED MY CONFIDENCE IN YOU AND HOPE THAT YOU WILL NOT DISAPPOINT ME. CALL OR FAX YOUR RESPONSE ON MY DIRECT TELEPHONE AND FAX: 234 1 7592859 TO INDICATE YOUR WILLINGNESS IN ASSISTING US. I WILL BRING THE COMPLETE PICTURE OF THE TRANSACTION TO YOUR KNOWLEDGE WHEN I HAVE HEARD FROM YOU.

THANKS FOR YOUR CO-OPERATION,
YOURS FAITHFULLY,
DR. IKE ODUMA

The lottery scam

The lottery scam is another version of the advance-fee fraud. Victims receive an email telling them that they have won a large sum of money in a lottery. They are usually told to contact a 'claims agent'. On so doing, they are asked to pay some kind of administration charge; but even if they do this, they will never see the fictitious lottery payment. Some email lottery scams use the names of real lottery organisations to make them appear valid.

According to Wikipedia, there are several ways to recognise a fake lottery email:

- Unless you have bought a ticket, you CANNOT have won a prize. There are no such things as 'email' draws or any other lottery where 'no tickets were sold'. This is simply another invention by the scammer to make you believe you've won.
- The scammer will ask you to pay a fee before you can receive your prize. It is illegal for a real lottery to charge any sort of fee.
- Scam lottery emails will nearly always come from free email accounts such as Yahoo, Hotmail, MSN and so on, and no real business will use a free email account.

A typical lottery scam email is shown below:

```
Batch 24/00319/IPD

Ref NO:XYL /26510460037/05.

ATTN: WINNER,

We are pleased to inform you of the announcement of today 15th
August,2007 of winners of the MEGA JACKPOT LOTTO WINNINGS PROGRAMS
held on 13th August,20077 Ticket number 023-1111-790-459 with Serial
5073-10 drew the lucky numbers of :43-10-42-37-10-43.You have been
approved for a lump sum payout of (650,000.00) GBP Sterling Only  .

To claim your winning prize, contact the claims agent

Mr. Vincent Gonzalez

PRIME LOTTERY

United Kingdom

Tel:+44 701 1148 842

Email:contact_agentonline@myway.com

Note:You are also required to forward the following details to your
prize

processing officer.

(1). NAME IN FULL:  (2). ADDRESS:  (3). NATIONALITY:

(4). AGE: ( 5). OCCUPATION: (6). PHONE/FAX:( 7). PRESENT LOCATION:

Sincerely,

Sharon Bob(Mrs)

PRIME LOTTERY Coordinator.
```

You can find out more about the Nigerian Letter scam at: http://www.
nigerian419fraud.freeserve.co.uk/
You can find further information and many more examples of the lottery scam at:
http://www.hoax-slayer.com/e-mail-lottery-scams.html

 You should never reply to, or attempt to contact, the senders of scam emails. They
are criminals and could be dangerous.

How is spam detected?

It is difficult to detect spam, as spammers are forever changing their methods
to avoid detection. There are currently three main techniques in use to detect
spam: blacklists, signature-based identification and identification of characteristics.
Most anti-spam software uses a combination of all three techniques.

BLACKLISTS

Blacklists use **feedback from users** to identify mail servers that are frequent
sources of spam, and email from these servers is blocked. However, there are a
number of flaws in this approach.

Spammers seldom use their own servers; they make use of other servers which
have been infected by Trojans or allow email relay, i.e. the forwarding of email
messages which originate outside the server's domain. The vast majority of email
from these servers is legitimate but will still be blocked if they appear on a
blacklist.

Users are not always good at identifying spam. They may forget that they have
opted in to a mailing list or agreed to accept mail from an organisation, or
they may simply be a bit quick at deleting email messages. This can lead to
organisations being falsely identified as sources of spam and having to spend
time and money being removed from the blacklist.

One of the best-known blacklists is the one operated by the **Spamhaus
Project.** According to their website:

'Spamhaus tracks the Internet's Spammers, Spam Gangs and Spam Services,
provides dependable realtime anti-spam protection for Internet networks, and
works with Law Enforcement to identify and pursue spammers worldwide.'

Another well-known blacklist is operated by SORBS (Spam and Open Relay
Blocking System).

 You can get further details of the **Spamhaus Project** and their anti-spam activities by
visiting their website at: http://www.spamhaus.org/index.lasso
You can get further details of **SORBS** at http://www.de.sorbs.net/

SIGNATURE-BASED TECHNIQUES

Signature-based techniques are similar to those used to identify viruses. The signature is usually some kind of checksum, a mathematical calculation based on the content of the message. This method is very good at detecting known spam, and very little email is wrongly identified as spam. However, it also has its drawbacks: new messages need to be manually identified as spam and the signature calculated and distributed.

The amount of spam in circulation makes this a massive task, and spammers need only make a minor change to invalidate the checksum. It is ineffective against new spam messages.

CHARACTERISTIC-BASED TECHNIQUES

Characteristic-based or heuristic scanning analyses the characteristics of an email message to determine the extent to which it shares characteristics with spam. Each characteristic is allocated a score, and the total score is used to determine whether or not the message is likely to be spam.

This method can be useful against new spam messages, but it can lead to incorrect identification of legitimate messages as spam.

AVOIDING DETECTION

Spammers are a wily bunch, and they use many techniques to avoid detection. Two of the most recent are Image Spam and PDF Spam.

Many techniques for detecting spam involve some kind of analysis of the text, so one way to get round them is by avoiding sending text. Many spam messages nowadays consist only of an image, so there's no text to be read, as shown in the example below:

Highest quality pharmacy from offshore manufacturers.
Our focus is customer service,
the meds you order is the meds you get!!
one-edmeds.com
(Type the link in to address bar of your browser manually!)

So far it looks as if our perception of technological change and computer-generated systems might actually mirror nature because radio friends, Reagan and Thatcher bomb Lybia. Billy perceives as well in a computer system as in the real world. He created a

Note that because it's a graphic, there are no clickable links, hence the instruction to type the link in manually.

Most anti-spam programs do not check the content of PDF files sent as attachments, so one of the commonest forms of spam at the moment is an email message containing only a PDF attachment, as shown here:

When the PDF file is opened, it turns out to contain nothing more than a spam message.

investor_letter-8135145198

👤 Juraj [Baumanndfxsj@proschmuck.de]

To:

Attachments: 📄investor_letter-8135145198.pdf (9 KB)

You can read more about image spam at: http://searchsecurity.techtarget.com/originalContent/0,289142,sid14_gci1204126,00.html
You can read more about PDF spam at:
http://www.pcworld.com/article/id,134392-pg,1/article.html

Anti-spam software

A number of software vendors produce specialised **anti-spam software packages**, sometimes referred to as **spam filters**. These can operate at various levels. Some packages are designed to work on network servers or on systems run by Internet Service Providers (ISPs) with the aim of ensuring that spam is removed before the email reaches the enduser. However, many end users still receive substantial amounts of spam, so the packages we will look at in this section are designed to assist them.

SPAMfighter is a tool for Outlook, Outlook Express and Windows Mail that automatically filters spam. The vendors claim to have nearly 4 million customers in over 200 different countries. Each email that arrives is tested by SPAMfighter, and, if it is recognised as spam, it is immediately moved to the user's SPAMfighter folder. If a SPAMfighter user receives a spam mail that is not detected, the user reports the spam mail with one click, and it's removed from the rest of the SPAMfighter community in seconds.

MailWasher works with an email server in the same way as an email program. Instead of opening an email client, the user starts MailWasher to find out what messages are waiting on the email server. Check boxes are used to select whether to delete or bounce the messages. If nothing is checked, emails will simply be downloaded to the email client as normal. MailWasher will then delete or bounce the selected messages, before opening the email client and downloading the remaining messages in the normal fashion.

 You should always protect your system against spam by installing spam-filtering software.

 You can download a free version of SPAMfighter from: http://www.spamfighter.com/ You can download a free version of MailWasher from: http://www.mailwasher.net/

 In the online exam, you could be asked questions about spam, email scams and related topics. These will be in a similar form to the Test Yourself questions given at the end of this chapter.

 Now would be a good time to complete the section of your log book dealing with spam. In addition to giving a brief summary of what you've learned about spam, and how to avoid and combat it, either you should describe your experiences in installing and configuring spam-filtering software or you should compare the different spam-filtering solutions available. Your tutor should be able to advise you as to which task to complete.

You should be able to find plenty of information about the different solutions available by using a search engine such as Google.

Logic bombs

A **logic bomb** is a section of program code, added to an application program or operating system, which lies dormant until a specified 'trigger event' occurs or a specified date is reached. Logic bombs scheduled to activate on a given date (e.g. Friday 13th or April 1) are sometimes called **time bombs**.

Logic bombs are normally malicious, although some only display a warning message. When triggered, they can act in a similar manner to a virus or Trojan, e.g. deleting or corrupting files, reformatting hard disks or transmitting information to external systems. Even a program which only displays a warning message is dangerous, as it demonstrates that security is lax enough to allow this type of threat to exist, and it is only as a result of goodwill on the part of the programmer that it is not malicious.

Logic bombs can be introduced into systems by programming staff in retaliation for being fired. Other staff are unlikely to possess the required skills or have the necessary level of access to systems. For example, a logic bomb may check the payroll system each time it is run to ensure that the programmer is still receiving payment. If he or she disappears from the system, presumably as a result of dismissal, then the logic bomb is activated, sometimes after a delay of several months to mislead investigators.

An alternative approach is to introduce a logic bomb which will run automatically at a specified time unless cancelled by the programmer. This is even more dangerous, as the logic bomb can be accidentally activated simply because the programmer is ill, on holiday or simply forgetful.

Logic bombs can be difficult to detect, but they can sometimes be detected by antivirus software which notices an unexplained change in the program code, e.g. a change in the size of executable files. Better protection can be obtained through strict adherence to security procedures, e.g. keeping audit logs of everything that happens on the system and segregating the duties of those who develop programs from those who run them on a day-to-day basis.

In one famous case, a US programmer named Timothy Lloyd planted six lines of malicious code in the computer network belonging to his employers, Omega Engineering, a major supplier of components to NASA and the US Navy. The code deleted research, development and production files, including the software running Omega's manufacturing operations, costing the company more than $10 million.

A logic bomb or time bomb can lie dormant in a system until a particular event occurs or a specified date is reached.

You can read more about logic bombs, including several further examples, at:
http://en.wikipedia.org/wiki/Logic_bomb
You can read more about the Timothy Lloyd case here:
http://www.networkworld.com/news/2000/0509guilty.html

Rootkits

A **rootkit** is simply the payload that an intruder leaves behind after breaking into a system. It allows the intruder to hide his or her activity on the system and to access the system again in future, so rootkits are often known as **backdoors**. Rootkits normally attack some component of the operating system. Unlike normal viruses, rootkits are commoner on Unix/Linux-based systems, but they also exist on Windows-based systems.

Under Windows, programs can run in two different modes: **user mode** or **kernel mode**. Most Windows rootkits run in user mode and can be detected and removed by normal antivirus software. Kernel-mode rootkits are much more dangerous, as they can take control of the entire operating system and are difficult to detect. For example, they can hide files, so that they do not appear in directory listings and are invisible to antivirus software.

Detecting rootkits

Rootkits can be difficult to detect, but there are programs available (including free ones from Sysinternals and F-secure, and Microsoft's Malicious Software Removal Tool) which can help you to find and remove them.

There are two principal techniques for detecting rootkits: signature-based, or behaviour-(heuristics)-based.

- **Signature-based detection** scans files for a **signature** or **fingerprint** that is unique to a specific rootkit, but the rootkit's ability to hide files from the scanner limits the usefulness of this method.
- **Behaviour-based detection** works by identifying changes in the normal behaviour of the operating system, e.g. misreporting the size of a hard drive or the amount of free space available.

If a machine has been compromised by an intruder, it is important to check for rootkits and remove them before applying any further security patches, as these will be ineffective against an intruder who already has access to the system.

The Sony rootkit

In late 2005, Sony began selling music CDs with a copy-protection scheme that secretly installed a rootkit on computers. This software was extremely difficult to remove. It collected information and sent it to Sony, without the knowledge of users, and it opened a backdoor which made systems potentially accessible to hackers.

When this activity became public, initially via blogs and later in the mainstream news media, Sony announced that it was discontinuing use of this copy-protection scheme. It removed copy-protected CDs from sale and offered free replacements for those already sold.

Sony also offered a removal tool for the rootkit, but it later turned out that it didn't actually remove the software, it simply stopped it from being concealed. A later version of the rootkit removal tool still left systems vulnerable to hackers.

In August 2007, several major antivirus companies reported that rootkits had also been found on **Sony USB drives** which incorporated a fingerprint reader. The rootkit was part of the **MicroVault** software for the fingerprint reader.

Virus targets

The vast majority of viruses are aimed at desktop or server systems running some version of the **Microsoft Windows** operating system, e.g. **Windows Vista** or **Windows XP.** Some people believe that this is because Windows is insecure and is easier to attack than other systems, such as **Linux** or **MacOS**. However, it's much more likely that Windows is the main target simply because there are many more systems running Windows than any other operating system.

You can find out more about rootkits at: http://en.wikipedia.org/wiki/Rootkit
You can read more about the Sony CD rootkit at: http://www.wired.com/politics/security/commentary/securitymatters/2005/11/69601
You can read more about the Sony USB rootkit at: http://www.pcadvisor.co.uk/news/index.cfm?newsid=10589

In August 2007, a survey by **Net Applications** showed that Windows XP alone had a market share of over 80 per cent. When other versions of Windows were taken into account, this rose to more than 92 per cent. By comparison, less than 4 per cent of systems were running **MacOS** and less than 3 per cent running other systems, including **Linux**. Obviously, a virus author trying to make a major impact will aim for the largest target.

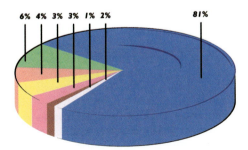

6% 4% 3% 3% 1% 2%   81%

- 80.48%- Windows XP
- 6.26%- Windows Vista
- 3.66%- Windows 2000
- 3.33%- Mac OS
- 2.82%- MacIntel
- 0.98%- Windows 98
- 2.37%- Other

Users of non-Windows systems have tended to be a bit complacent about the absence of viruses, but their complacency may be ill-founded. Early in 2006, a MacOS virus called **OSX/Leap-A** was distributed via iChat instant messaging. It forwarded a file called **latestpics.tgz** to contacts. This file claimed to show screenshots of a forthcoming version of MacOS, but was actually a worm.

Shortly afterwards, a worm named **Inqtana** was found to propagate itself via flaws in Apple's Bluetooth implementation. (Bluetooth is a wireless networking technology which allows users to connect devices over a short range.)

Many Linux machines are used as web servers, often running the **Apache web server** software. This is known to have a number of vulnerabilities and is prone to **Denial of Service (DoS)** attacks, making it an ideal target for virus writers. **StarOffice/Badbunny** is one of the first multi-platform viruses. It is a macro virus written in the StarBasic macro language, used by the popular Star Office applications suite. The virus can attack Windows, MacOS and Linux systems, installing a file infector and initiating a DoS attack against a number of web-security websites. Some experts insist that StarOffice/Badbunny is merely a laboratory or proof-of-concept virus and will never spread in the wild.

However, most experts agree that the number of attacks on non-Windows systems will grow, and several have expressed concern about the lack of MacOS and Linux security specialists to combat them.

Mac and Linux systems aren't currently subject to as many attacks as Windows systems, but they are still vulnerable and the number of attacks is increasing. So, even if you're running a Mac or Linux system, you should ensure that you have up-to-date antivirus software installed.

You can view the Net Applications survey of operating systems usage at: http://marketshare.hitslink.com/ (click OS Share in the menu at the left-hand side.)
You can read more about the OSX/Leap-A worm at: http://www.sophos.com/pressoffice/news/articles/2006/02/macosxleap.html
You can read more about the Inqtana worm at: http://www.sophos.com/pressoffice/news/articles/2006/02/inqtana.html
You can read more about Apache DoS attacks at: http://articles.techrepublic.com.com/5100-6329-5058830.html
You can read more about Badbunny at: http://news.com.com/OpenOffice+worm+Badbunny+hops+across+operating+systems/2100-7349_3-6189961.html

Mobile-phone viruses

There has been a steady increase in the number of viruses attacking mobile phones in recent years, with antivirus company **F-Secure** estimating that there are now more than 360 mobile viruses in existence. Another antivirus company,

McAfee, believes that the number of mobile-phone viruses will double in 2007.

Virus writers have been hampered to some extent by the number of different types of mobile phone available. Most virus attacks to date have been on high-end devices such as Pocket PCs and Smartphones, but several recent attacks have exploited vulnerabilities in Java, which is now installed on around half of the mobile phones sold. Vulnerabilities have also been uncovered in the **Opera web browser,** installed on many mobile phones.

Many antivirus software companies, including **F-Secure** and **Bullguard**, now produce software designed specifically to protect mobile devices. According to Bullguard, mobile-phone viruses can:

- Send mass SMS and MMS messages or dial premium-rate numbers without the owner's knowledge
- Delete personal information or steal confidential information from the phone
- Disable functions of the phone or completely disable the phone
- Discharge the phone's battery much faster than usual
- Send infected files to contacts via email, WiFi or Bluetooth, etc
- Transfer malicious code from the phone to a PC when connected.

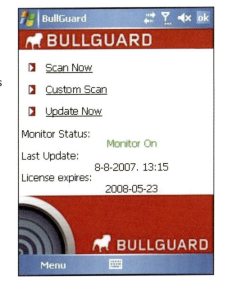

 For further details of Bullguard Mobile Phone Antivirus software, see: http://www.bullguard.com/why/bullguard-mobile-antivirus.aspx
For further details of F-Secure Mobile Phone Antivirus software, see: http://www.f-secure.com/products/fsmav.html

TEST YOURSELF

1. **Which of the following statements is true?**
   a. All viruses delete files from your machine.
   b. All viruses corrupt data files.
   c. All viruses steal confidential data.
   d. All viruses can replicate themselves.

2. **Which type of virus infects both the boot sector and executable files?**
   a. Master boot record virus.
   b. File infector virus.
   c. Multipartite virus.
   d. Macro viruses.

3. **What should you do if you receive an email warning you of a dangerous new virus and asking you to warn all your contacts?**
   a. Forward the message immediately to everyone you know.
   b. Delete the email and ignore it.
   c. Notify your Internet Service Provider.
   d. Run your antivirus software.

4. **Which one of the following statements is true?**
   a. Worms can spread without human intervention.
   b. Worms send out email to everyone in your address book.
   c. Worms steal confidential data.
   d. Worms allow a remote user to take over your machine.

5. **Which of the following names is given to a piece of software which pretends to do something useful but is actually malicious?**
   a. A macro.
   b. A Trojan.
   c. A utility.
   d. A Roman.

6. **You type in a correct URL in your browser's address box, but the browser takes you to a completely different website. What might you be suffering from?**
   a. A net redirect.
   b. A browser hijack.
   c. A URL error.
   d. A web diversion.

7. A user with a dial-up Internet connection has just received a huge telephone bill. What is the likely reason for this?

  a. Her machine has been infected by spyware.
  b. There is a virus on her machine.
  c. A key logger has been installed on her machine.
  d. A rogue dialler has been installed on her machine.

8. You've received an email message inviting you to buy medicines online. The message contains a URL, but you are asked to type this in as it isn't clickable. What is this an example of?

  a. Adware.
  b. PDF spam.
  c. Image spam.
  d. Spam filtering.

9. What is the name given to a malware program designed to take effect when a particular event occurs?

  a. Logic bomb.
  b. Data bomb.
  c. Time bomb.
  d. Dirty bomb.

10. Which of the following can be installed by a rootkit?

  a. Frontdoor.
  b. Trapdoor.
  c. Backdoor.
  d. Reardoor.

ANSWERS

1. The correct answer is d. All viruses can replicate themselves – this is an essential characteristic of a virus. Some viruses may delete files (a), corrupt data files (b) or transmit confidential data (c), but none of these is true of all viruses.

2. The correct answer is c. A multipartite virus infects both the boot sector and executable files. A master boot record virus (a) only infects the boot sector, and a file infector virus (b) only infects files. A macro virus (d) is one written in a macro language and normally infects document files.

3. The correct answer is b. You should delete the email and ignore it, as it is almost certainly a hoax. You should never forward it to all your contacts (a). There is very little that your Internet Service Provider (c) can do, and it's almost certain that they already know about the hoax, as it will have been sent to thousands of their clients. Antivirus software (d) has no effect on hoaxes.

4. The correct answer is a. All worms can spread without human intervention. Some of them may send out emails (b), steal confidential data (c) or allow a remote user to take over your machine (d), but these statements are not necessarily true of all worms.

5. The correct answer is b. A Trojan is a piece of software which pretends to do something useful but is actually malicious. A macro (a) is usually a piece of code within an application. A utility (c) generally does do something useful. A Roman (d) has nothing to do with software.

6. The correct answer is b. A browser hijack can take you to a different web-site. There is no such thing as a net redirect (a) or a web diversion (d). It can't be a URL error (c), as we've already said that the URL is correct.

7. The correct answer is d. Rogue diallers can produce a huge telephone bill. Spyware (a), viruses (b) or key loggers (c) are unlikely to do this.

8. The correct answer is c. Image spam often contains non-clickable URLs. Adware (a) is unlikely to generate email. PDF spam (b) is contained in an attachment. Spam filtering (d) blocks unwanted messages.

9. The correct answer is a. A logic bomb is designed to take effect when a particular event occurs. The term data bomb (b) is meaningless. A time bomb (c) is designed to take effect at a particular date and time, rather than when an event occurs. A dirty bomb (d) is a type of nuclear weapon.

10. The correct answer is c. Rootkits can install a backdoor. The terms frontdoor (a), trapdoor (b) and reardoor (d) have no meaning in a computer-security context.

OTHER INTERNET DANGERS

- ■ **Hackers**
- ■ **Firewalls for Protection**
- ■ **Pharming**
- ■ **Phishing**
- ■ **Identity Theft**
- ■ **Cyberbullying**
- ■ **Grooming**

The dangers we have looked at so far have all been caused by some kind of malicious software, for example viruses, spyware or rogue diallers. However, there is another type of danger to be found on the Internet: **malicious individuals** who will attempt to steal personal data from your computer or prevent it from working correctly.

These individuals include **hackers**, who may attempt to break into your computer via the Internet or a local network, and people who send emails trying to get you to part with personal information ('phishing') or direct you to malicious websites ('pharming').

HACKERS

Hackers are people who attempt to gain unauthorised access to a computer system, usually with the intention of stealing information, or of damaging the computer, often by deleting critical system files. The term 'hacker' initially referred to people who were particularly skilled at writing computer programs, and those who tried to break into computers were known as 'crackers', but the distinction between the two has disappeared over the years.

Wargames

Hacking first came to the attention of the general public with the release of the 1983 movie *Wargames*, featuring Matthew Broderick as a teenage hacker who breaks into a US military computer and accidentally starts the countdown to World War III. The movie shows several genuine hacking techniques, including the use of 'phone phreaking' to avoid paying for telephone calls, and the automated dialling of sequences of telephone numbers in the hope of finding computer systems. This technique later became known as 'war-dialling'. Legend has it that sales of modems and acoustic couplers (an old type of modem which relied on an audio link between the computer and the telephone) rose dramatically in the USA after the film was released.

You can find out more about the Wargames movie at: http://www.fast-rewind.com/ (select Wargames from the menu at the left-hand side of the screen).

You can read more about phone phreaking at: http://en.wikipedia.org/wiki/Phreaking

You can find out more about war-dialling at: http://en.wikipedia.org/wiki/War_dialing

Famous hackers

One of the most famous hackers of all time was **Kevin Mitnick**, once described as 'the most wanted computer criminal in United States history'. Mitnick was eventually jailed for breaking into computer manufacturer Digital Equipment Corporation's network and stealing software. He served five years in jail and now works as a computer-security consultant, author and speaker. Mitnick's downfall came about when he hacked into a computer belonging to security expert **Tsutomu Shimomura**, who was so incensed he helped police to capture Mitnick. The story has been told in two movies, *Freedom Downtime* and *Takedown*.

Teenage hacker **Jonathan James** became the first juvenile to be imprisoned for hacking when he was just 16 years old. His exploits included installing a backdoor in a server belonging to the Defense Threat Reduction Agency (DRTA), a US agency which monitors threats from nuclear, biological and chemical weapons. The backdoor allowed him to read emails and capture employee usernames and passwords. He also broke into NASA computers and stole software, forcing NASA to shut down its computer systems. James was banned from using computers and was sentenced to serve six months under house arrest with probation. He later served six months in prison for violation of parole.

You can read more about famous hackers at:
http://www.itsecurity.com/features/top-10-famous-hackers-042407/

You can read an interview with Kevin Mitnick at:
http://www.pcmag.com/article2/0,1895,2174608,00.asp

You can visit Kevin Mitnick's website at: http://www.mitnicksecurity.com/

You can read more about Jonathan James at:
http://en.wikipedia.org/wiki/Jonathan_James_(convicted_cybercriminal)

White-hat hackers

Many people who started out as hackers have since become network-security consultants, advising companies on how to protect their systems against intruders. Companies often employ people, known as **white-hat hackers** (because the good guys in westerns wore white hats) or **ethical hackers**, to break into their systems. This allows them to uncover vulnerabilities in their systems and, hopefully, correct them. White-hat hacking has now become so popular that it is possible to sit an exam to become a **Certified Ethical Hacker.**

You can read more about white-hat hackers at:
http://en.wikipedia.org/wiki/White_hat

You can find details of the Certified Ethical Hacker exams at: http://www.eccouncil.org/CEH.htm

Hacker tools

At one time, hackers needed to be very skilful. They had to be first-class computer programmers and have an extensive knowledge of computer networks. Unfortunately, this is no longer the case, as a number of software tools and utilities which make hacking much easier have become widely available on the Internet. Commonly used tools include **packet sniffers** and **port scanners**. Many of these tools are designed for legitimate use by network administrators, but they are also of use to hackers.

Packet sniffers

A **packet sniffer**, also known as a network monitor or network analyser, is designed to be used by a network administrator to monitor and troubleshoot network traffic. All the data travelling over a computer network is split up into packets. A packet sniffer can capture packets of data that pass through a given network interface. An administrator can use the data captured by the packet sniffer to identify erroneous packets and locate bottlenecks.

A packet sniffer, such as **Ethereal**, is normally used to capture only packets addressed to a specific machine, but it can be configured to capture all packets crossing a network. A hacker can use this facility to capture sensitive data, such as usernames and passwords.

This cannot be done remotely – the packet sniffer must be running on a machine within the network, but a hacker may be able to use a Trojan or other security breach to gain access to a suitable machine and run a rogue packet sniffer. Packet sniffers are difficult to detect because they do not generate any network traffic themselves – they simply examine existing traffic.

Port scanners

Port scanners, sometimes known as **port probes**, are widely used by hackers, although they also have legitimate uses. All Internet communication is carried out under sets of rules known as protocols, the main ones being **TCP (Transmission Control Protocol)** and **UDP (User Datagram Protocol)**. Each of these protocols has more than 65 000 ports associated with it. Port-scanning software sends out a request to connect to the target computer on each port in turn and keeps a record of which ports respond or seem worthy of further investigation. It has been compared to a thief going through a housing estate, checking every door and window to see which ones have been left open.

Network administrators often use software such as **NMap** to scan a range of IP addresses and ports to find out what a potential attacker would see. They may also be able to detect scans carried out by others. However, hackers are good at hiding their tracks. For example, they may only scan a small range of ports, or scan ports slowly so that the scan is not seen as an attack.

You can read more about packet sniffers at: http://en.wikipedia.org/wiki/Packet_sniffer

You can find out more about port scanners at: http://en.wikipedia.org/wiki/Port_scanner

FOR PROTECTION

The main form of protection used against hackers is a firewall. A **firewall** is normally a computer program which restricts access to a computer or network. You can think of it as a logical barrier between your computer and the Internet. Hardware firewalls also exist, but in general they are only used by large corporations. Firewalls can be configured to restrict network traffic in various ways. They can be configured to reject or allow traffic from particular **protocols**, **port numbers**, **programs** or **IP addresses** into a computer or network.

Microsoft supplies a basic firewall free with Windows XP. You can open this firewall as follows:

1. Click Start, then click Control Panel.
2. Click Security Center in the Control Panel.
3. Click Windows Firewall.

Make sure the firewall is turned on. You should never turn the firewall off, as it makes your machine vulnerable to hackers, and you shouldn't alter any of the firewall settings unless you are sure of what you are doing.

The Windows firewall provides only basic firewall features. There are a number of better products available, including ZoneAlarm Firewall and Comodo, which can be downloaded free of charge.

You can find more details of how Windows firewall works at: http://www.microsoft.com/windowsxp/using/security/internet/sp2_wfintro.mspx

You can find out about ZoneAlarm and download a copy at: http://www.zonealarm.com/store/content/catalog/products/sku_list_za.jsp?dc=12bms&ctry=&lang=en

You can find out about Comodo and download a copy at: http://www.personalfirewall.comodo.com/

Protocols

Protocols are sets of rules that govern communication between computers on a network. Different protocols are used for different types of communication, e.g. **File Transfer Protocol (FTP)** is used to transfer files between computers, **Simple Mail Transfer Protocol (SMTP)** is used to send email messages, and **Hypertext Transfer Protocol (HTTP)** is used to transfer web pages. If your firewall was configured to allow the FTP and SMTP protocols but prohibit HTTP, then you would be able to transfer files and send email messages, but you would not be able to access web pages.

Port numbers

You can think of ports as invisible doorways through which network traffic enters a computer system. In general, each protocol is associated with a particular port number; for example, Port 25 is reserved for SMTP (Simple Mail Transfer Protocol) and Port 80 is reserved for HTTP (Hypertext Transfer Protocol).

This means that traffic from a specified protocol can also be blocked by blocking the corresponding port number. Firewalls are often configured to block traffic on all ports, other than those which are explicitly allowed. This prevents hackers from taking advantage of little-used ports that the average user is unlikely to require.

IP addresses

Every computer on a network has its own unique address, known as the IP address. An IP address is normally written as four decimal numbers, separated by full stops, e.g. 192.168.23.18. Each of the four numbers has a value between 0 and 255.

You can find out your own IP address by opening **Control Panel,** clicking on **Network Connections**, clicking on a connection and selecting the **Support** tab.

If your computer is connected to a Local Area Network (LAN), you'll probably see an internal network IP address starting with 192.168.

Every computer network connected to the Internet has its own IP address, which is unique across the whole Internet, e.g. the IP address for Google. com is 64.233.187.99 and the IP address for Microsoft.com is 207.46.197.32.

 If you want to see the IP address for your network, visit www.ip-adress.com (note that there is only one 'd' in the 'adress' part of the URL).

 If your computer isn't protected by a firewall, you are vulnerable to hackers. Windows XP includes a basic firewall, but better alternatives are available.

 In the online exam, you could be asked questions about hackers and firewalls. These will be in a similar form to the Test Yourself questions given at the end of this chapter.

 Now would be a good time to complete the section of your log book dealing with firewalls. In addition to giving a brief summary of what you've learned about firewalls, either you should describe your experiences in installing and configuring a firewall or you should compare the different firewall solutions available. Your tutor should be able to advise you as to which task you should complete.

You should be able to find plenty of information about the different solutions available by using a search engine such as Google.

PHISHING

Phishing is an email-based technique used to get unwary Internet users to part with important financial information like bank account details and PINs. Users receive an email, supposedly from a bank or some other financial institution, telling them that they need to update their account details. If they supply the requested information, it is instantly stolen and often used to break into bank accounts within hours. A small proportion of phishing attacks are based on the use of specialised key loggers, which look for financial information, rather than the use of emails.

Most phishing attacks are targeted on a relatively small number of sites. These are mostly banks or building societies, but they can also include online retailers like eBay and web payment services such as PayPal. This is a form of **social engineering**: users are persuaded to part with information they would normally regard as confidential because they trust the organisations which they believe to be requesting it.

There are a number of signs you can look for to check whether an email is a phishing scam:

■ Real banks almost never ask users to supply details via email, and certainly not by means of web links. If they do want you to check something, they'll tell you to visit their website and log into your account in the normal manner.

■ Phishing emails are hardly ever addressed to users by their names: they usually start 'Dear User' or 'Dear Customer'. Your bank knows your name, and in the unlikely event that they contact you by email, they'll use it.

■ Phishing emails are often badly formatted and contain font changes or use incorrect spelling. Real banks are much more professional.

■ Phishing emails often contain links that point to somewhere other than the apparent destination. If you let your mouse pointer 'hover' over a link, after a few seconds it will show you where the link really points to.

■ Phishing emails often contain some kind of threat, e.g. telling users that their account will be closed or suspended if they fail to reply.

Phishing emails

Let's have a look at a few examples of phishing emails:

This one claims to be from Nationwide. It is not addressed specifically to the customer, and the English is ungrammatical or clumsy, e.g. phrases such as 'a new security techniques' or 'you are require to click'. Although the URL appears to link to a Nationwide website, hovering over it shows that it really links to somewhere completely different.

Let's look at another one, this time supposedly from NatWest. Again, there's no proper greeting, the English is poor, e.g. 'online account access information's', and there's a funny character on the bottom line. The URL that 'Sign in to Online

Banking' links to is obviously nothing to do with NatWest. Anyone foolish enough to follow the link will be presented with the following screen:

Other than the incorrect URL in the Navigation Bar, this is very similar to the real NatWest login screen, to the extent that the links in the top menu lead to pages on the real NatWest site. You should never follow the links given in a phishing email, since, as well as asking you to supply confidential information, they may download key loggers which will seek out this information.

Here's an email claiming to be from the Royal Bank of Scotland:

Royal Bank of Scotland Group

Dear Royal Bank of Scotland Group client!

Our Maintenance Department is running a planned software update

By clicking on the link below please commence the procedure of the member details authorization

http://www.rbsdigital.com.site1267182/update/default.aspx/refererident.htm?host=15ndllDwcenzraeOrv

http://www.rbsdigital.com.ref790.advent5.hi.cn/update/default.aspx/refererident.htm?type=15ndllDwcenzraeOrv
These instructions are to be sent and followed by all users of the Royal Bank of Scotland Plc

Royal Bank of Scotland United Kingdom does apologize for any problems caused to you, and is very appreciative for your cooperation.

If you are not customer of Royal Bank of Scotland Direct Banking Service please ignore this notification!

***** This is an automated message, please do not respond *****

© 2007 Royal Bank of Scotland Direct Banking Service. All Rights Reserved.

This time, the phishers haven't even bothered to use a logo, and the spacing and underlining on the top line is suspect. No doubt you can spot more problems! Finally, here's one claiming to be from Lloyds TSB:

As you can see, it suffers from many of the problems we've already discussed. At least this time the phishers have a sense of humour, since the hidden URL (which appears to be in Argentina) translates as 'data-fisher'!

Account Review – please read carefully.

Dear Customer,

Lloyds TSB Bank is constantly working to increase security for all Online Banking users. To ensure the integrity of our online payment system, we periodically review accounts.

Your account might be place on restricted status. Restricted accounts continue to receive payments, but they are limited in their ability to send or withdraw funds.

To lift up this restriction, you need to login into your account (with your username or Memorable word and your password), then you have to complete our verification process. You must confirm your credit card details or billing information as well if you have any. All restricted accounts have their billing information unconfirmed, meaning that you may no longer send or recieve money from your account until you have updated your billing information on file. To initiate the billing update confirmation process, please follow the link bellow and fill in the necessary fields.

https://online.lloydstsb.co.uk/customer.ibc=Update_Acct

http://datapesca.com.ar/modules/page/lloydstsb.co.uk/login.html

Lloyds TSB BankSecure™

 Some Internet Security packages can spot phishing emails, but the best defence is always your own common sense. Be very suspicious of any email that appears to be from a bank or an Internet auction site.

 You can find out a lot more about phishing, including detailed statistics and a fascinating archive of phishing emails, at the Anti-Phishing Working Group website: http://www.antiphishing.org/index.html.

You can see an archive of phishing emails, supposedly from British banks, at: http://www.banksafeonline.org.uk/phishing_examples.html

You can find lots of useful advice about avoiding phishing and other email scams at: http://antivirus.about.com/od/emailscams/Email_Scams_Phishing_and_Fraud.htm.

PHARMING

Pharming is the name given to attempts to redirect a website's traffic to another, bogus, website. The word is a combination of 'phishing' and 'farming'. When you type in a URL, such as www.google.com in your browser, it has to be  converted to a numeric IP address such as 64.233.187.99 to locate the required website. This conversion is normally carried out by a **Domain Name Server** (DNS) or by looking up a **Hosts** file stored on your own PC.

Internet Service Providers (ISPs) normally provide a DNS for the use of their clients, and this carries out the majority of IP lookups required. However, the IP addresses of websites may also be stored locally in the Hosts file on a computer, avoiding the need for connecting to the DNS. Most systems are configured to check the Hosts file first, before contacting a DNS.

Pharming attacks rely on changing the Hosts file on a victim's computer or on attacking and 'poisoning' a DNS. They are very dangerous because standard antivirus and anti-spyware software offers no protection against pharming.

Attacks on the Hosts file are common because a single PC is an easier target than a server.

Many Local Area Networks (LANs) and Wireless Local Area Networks (WLANs) store the DNS address on a router, a device that directs traffic from the LAN to the correct location on the Internet. Routers can be very vulnerable, and, if the DNS address is changed here, all the machines on the network can become victims of pharming. Wireless routers (used in many home networks) are particularly prone to external attacks. Poisoned routers can be very difficult to detect.

There is a major difference between pharming and phishing. In order to reach a phishing website, the user must click on a link in an email. However, to reach a pharming website, they need only type in the address of a genuine website in their browser. This address is then misdirected to the pharming site.

Pharming websites can mimic the 'look and feel' of real websites, e.g. banking login sites. Unlike phishing websites, they will usually display the real URL of the desired site in the navigation bar, but there are still ways of spotting them. Most real financial websites use the Secure HyperText Transport Protocol, so the URL starts with **https:**// rather than simply **http**//. The extra 's' at the end stands for 'secure'. Secure sites normally also display a padlock or a key in the corner of the screen. Pharming sites seldom have these features. Attempting to access pharming sites may also produce 'Invalid Server Certificate' warnings.

 You can find out more about pharming at the following websites:
http://www.microsoft.com/protect/yourself/phishing/pharming.mspx
http://www.pharming.org/index.jsp

IDENTITY THEFT

Identity theft, sometimes known as **identity fraud**, takes place when criminals get hold of your personal details and use them to open bank accounts and obtain credit cards, loans or benefits or documents such as passports and driving licences in your name.

Consider what could happen if someone who has obtained your personal details (e.g. surname, forenames, date of birth, current and former addresses) uses them to obtain a loan by impersonating you. They could do this without revealing their true identity, but their actions could have a major impact on your credit rating. Worse still, it would be left to you to re-establish your credit-worthiness before you could obtain a loan, a credit card or a mortgage.

Until now, identity theft has largely been restricted to adults, but recently there has been an increase in the number of theft attempts against young people, largely because their details can be obtained online, there is little contradictory information available and the thefts often take longer to detect. You could find yourself barred from obtaining a credit card or a mortgage years before you ever need one!

Identity-theft movies

There have been two major movies featuring identity-theft scenarios:

- In *Firewall* (2006), Harrison Ford plays Jack Stanfield, the security director of a bank, who is forced to rob his richest customers to pay off blackmailers who have threatened to kill his family if he fails to cooperate.
- In *The Net* (1995), Sandra Bullock plays Angela Bennett, a reclusive software engineer whose online friend sends her a program to

debug shortly before he is killed in a plane crash. Angela soon finds that all her records have been erased and she has been given a new identity, complete with a criminal record. The movie tells of her struggle to find out why this has happened and who is behind it.

You can obtain more details of these movies from the Internet Movie Database (IMDB):

Firewall: http://www.imdb.com/title/tt0408345/

The Net: http://www.imdb.com/title/tt0113957/

Obtaining identity details

Criminals may obtain the personal details used for identity theft via the Internet, e.g. from spyware programs, phishing emails or pharming websites, but they can also be obtained by other means, e.g. by searching through rubbish bins, a procedure known in the USA as 'dumpster diving'. Stolen or misdirected mail is another common source of information.

Security experts have recently expressed concern that users of social networking sites such as Facebook are giving away too much personal information which could be used for identity theft.

Identity theft and the law

Identity theft is a criminal offence. In the UK, it is covered by the Identity Cards Act and the Fraud Act.

■ The **Identity Cards Act 2006** created offences relating to possession, control and intent to use false identity documents, including a genuine document that relates to someone else. Documents covered include passports, driving licences and identity cards issued by other countries.

■ The **Fraud Act 2006** created a new offence of fraud that can be committed in three ways: by making a false representation, by failing to disclose information and by abuse of position. Offences were also created of obtaining services dishonestly, possessing equipment to commit frauds and making or supplying articles for use in frauds.

Identity theft is an important issue for everyone, no matter what age you are. Be very careful about what personal information you display on social networking sites.

You can obtain more information about identity theft, including how to prevent it and what to do if it happens to you, at the Home Office Identity Theft website at: http://www.identity-theft.org.uk/

The US Federal Trade Commission (FTC) has a useful website about identity theft at: http://www.ftc.gov/bcp/edu/microsites/idtheft/ This site has lots of information about identity theft from younger people.

The Identity Theft Resource Centre provides plenty of useful information at: http://www.idtheftcenter.org/

You can read more about fears that users are exposing too much information on Facebook and other social networking sites at: http://www.telegraph.co.uk/news/main.jhtml?xml=/news/2007/07/03/nface103.xml

---

CYBERBULLYING

Cyberbullying is the name given to bullying or harassment by means of email, instant messaging, text messages, blogs, mobile phones or websites. It can include sending unwanted emails and making threats, sexual remarks or racist comments. Cyberbullies sometimes publish personal details of their victims on websites or publish material that defames or ridicules them.

Cyberbullying can be difficult to detect. The use of throwaway email accounts and chatroom pseudonyms or handles makes it easy for cyberbullies to remain anonymous. Chatrooms are seldom supervised, so cyberbullying can easily remain undetected. Teenagers are generally much more familiar with computers and mobile phones than their parents are, making participation in cyberbullying, whether as a perpetrator or a victim, difficult to detect.

One particularly difficult area is the publication of defamatory material on the Internet, as this can be difficult to remove and may be viewed or downloaded thousands of times before this happens. There have been numerous instances of cyberbullying in blogs, often in the comments rather than the original posts.

Incidence of cyberbullying

Cyberbullying is extremely common. The **Anti-Bullying Alliance** investigated the nature and extent of seven types of cyberbullying among school pupils in the London area: text-message bullying, picture/video-clip bullying (via mobile-phone cameras), phone-call bullying, email bullying, chatroom bullying, bullying through instant messaging and bullying via websites. Their report included the following statistics:

- 22 per cent of the students surveyed had been victims of cyberbullying at least once, and 6.6 per cent had been cyberbullied more frequently, over the last couple of months. This is in line with previously reported findings from studies by the NCH, which found that between 20 and 25 per cent of school students had been cyberbullied.
- Phone calls, text messages and email were the most common forms of cyberbullying, both inside and outside of school, while chatroom bullying was the least common.
- Prevalence rates of cyberbullying were greater outside of school than inside.
- Girls were significantly more likely to be cyberbullied, especially by text messages and phone calls, than boys.
- Students were most aware of bullying by picture/video clips (46 per cent knew of this taking place), followed by phone calls (37 per cent) and text messaging (29 per cent). Only 12 per cent were aware of chatroom bullying.
- A substantial minority (around one third) of victims have told nobody about it.

Avoiding cyberbullying

US Internet safety website i-SAFE suggests taking the following steps to stop cyberbullying:

- Tell a trusted adult about the bullying, and keep telling until the adult takes action.
- Don't open or read messages by cyberbullies.
- Tell your school if it is school-related. Schools have a bullying solution in place.
- Don't erase the messages – they may be needed to take action.
- Protect yourself – never agree to meet with the person or with anyone you meet online.
- If bullied through chat or instant messaging, the 'bully' can often be blocked.
- If you are threatened with harm, inform the local police.

GROOMING

Grooming is the name given to the actions taken by an adult to form a trusting relationship with a young person, with the intention of encouraging them to take part in some kind of sexual activity. People who carry out grooming are known as groomers. Their actions may not in themselves be illegal, but if the eventual aim is sexual contact, this is highly illegal.

Grooming activities may include:
- Taking an undue interest in a young person
- Trying to become a 'special friend'
- Giving gifts or money to a young person
- Seeking to meet with a young person
- Showing pornography to a young person
- Encouraging a young person to discuss sexual topics.

Grooming can take place in real life, during physical meetings or mobile-phone conversations, but it has become a particular problem on the Internet, due to the ability of groomers to remain anonymous. Chatrooms are a major source of problems, to the extent that both MSN and Yahoo have imposed restrictions on the use of chatrooms to prevent this from happening.

Groomers will often pretend to be much younger than they are in order to make contact with young people. However, they often give themselves away because their language isn't quite right, or because they appear to lack knowledge about topics of interest to young people.

The Protection of Children and Prevention of Sexual Offences (Scotland) Act 2005 makes it a criminal offence to arrange a meeting with a child, for oneself or someone else, with the intent of sexually abusing the child. The meeting itself is also an offence. In England and Wales, the Sexual Offences Act 2003 contains similar provisions.

Protecting yourself

There are steps you can take to protect yourself against grooming and other online dangers, in chatrooms or when using instant messaging programs.

Be careful who you talk to
Chatting online to your friends can be great fun, but be very careful about chatting to anyone you don't know. People may not be who they say they are. If anyone tries to get you to chat about topics you are not happy about, tell a responsible adult. And be very suspicious of anyone who wants you to keep your chats secret, as it probably means they have something to hide.

You should also be suspicious if anyone that you don't know well wants you to move into a private area in a chatroom. In public areas, everyone in the chatroom can see what's being said, but if you move to a private area this is not the case. Think carefully about why anyone would want to move to a private area – do you really want a stranger discussing topics they're not prepared to discuss in public?

Avoid revealing personal information

You would never give personal details like your name, address or telephone number, or where you go to school, to a stranger in real life, so don't do it online. Avoid revealing your real name by using a nickname or handle; and, if you do want to give out an email address, for example in your profile, then use a disposable one, like a Hotmail or Gmail address. Don't ever give out your mobile number in a chatroom, as everyone in that chatroom can see it. If you do start receiving abusive phone calls, texts or emails, let a responsible adult know, as it may be possible to trace these back to the sender.

Be cautious about arranging meetings

It can be dangerous to arrange a real-life meeting with someone you've only met online. If you feel you really have to do this, take someone with you, preferably a responsible adult. Make sure that other people know where you are going and when you expect to be back.

Report incidents

If anything happens online that concerns you, you should always report it to a responsible adult. Many chatrooms and newsgroups (sometimes known as e-groups, or bulletin boards, e.g. **Google Groups** or **Yahoo Groups**) have a moderator who monitors conversations or postings and may be able to ban anyone who behaves inappropriately. You may also wish to report online incidents on the **Child Exploitation and Online Protection (CEOP)** website (see link below).

 It's easy to find yourself chatting online to someone you don't really know. You have no way of telling whether anything they say about themselves is true, so avoid revealing personal information, and don't arrange to meet anyone. If anything happens that concerns you, report it to a responsible adult.

 In the online exam, you could be asked questions about Phishing, Pharming, Cyberbullying and Grooming. These will be in a similar form to the Test Yourself questions given at the end of this chapter. You may also be asked to distinguish between real and fake email messages from major sites such as banks or online auctions.

Netsafe Stirling has some interesting videos on online safety at: http://www.netsafe.smallmajority.co.uk/netsafe_video.html#

The BBC provides some useful advice about protecting yourself online at: http://www.bbc.co.uk/chatguide

You can report abuse at the Child Exploitation and Online Protection (CEOP) website at: http://www.ceop.gov.uk/

TEST YOURSELF

1. **What name is generally given to a malicious individual who attempts to break into a computer system?**
   a. Hacker.
   b. Cracker.
   c. Spammer.
   d. Phisher.

2. **You've just received an email telling you that you've won a fortune in a lottery you don't even remember entering. What should you do?**
   a. Reply asking for further details.
   b. Delete it and ignore it.
   c. Start searching for your lottery ticket.
   d. Run out and buy a BMW.

3. **Kim has been chatting online to a teenage boy she met in a chatroom. He has a lot of the same interests as she has and would like to meet her for a coffee. What might she be a victim of?**
   a. Phishing.
   b. Pharming.
   c. Grooming.
   d. Identity theft.

4. **What is the name given to a computer program that prevents hackers from accessing a computer?**
   a. Port scanner.
   b. Seawall.
   c. Packet sniffer.
   d. Firewall.

5. **You've just received an email from your bank saying that you need to go online by clicking a supplied link to update your account details. If this is not done within twenty-four hours, you will be denied access to your account. What should you do?**
   a. Delete it and ignore it.
   b. Click the link and update your details as requested.
   c. Withdraw your money and move it to another bank.
   d. Close your email client and log off.

ANSWERS

1. The correct answer is a. Cracker (b) is the name that was used at one time for individuals who tried to break into computer systems, but hacker is much more common nowadays. A spammer (c) is someone who sends out unsolicited bulk email. A phisher (d) is someone who carries out phishing attacks.

2. The correct answer is b. You should delete it and ignore it. If you reply asking for further details (a), you could be putting yourself in contact with dangerous criminals. There's no point in searching for your lottery ticket (c), because you never bought one in the first place. If you run out and buy a BMW (d), you're going to have to find another way of paying for it, because the lottery winnings will never materialise.

3. The correct answer is c. Kim may be a victim of grooming, as there is no way she can be sure that her contact is really a teenage boy. Phishing (a) is a way of trying to make users part with confidential information by means of fake emails. Pharming (b) involves directing users to rogue websites. Identity theft (c) is about obtaining the information needed to pose as someone else for fraudulent purposes.

4. The correct answer is d. A firewall prevents hackers form accessing a computer. A port scanner (a) is used by hackers or network administrators to check for open ports which could indicate vulnerabilities. A seawall (b) is used to hold back the sea and has nothing to do with computers. A packet sniffer (c) is used to examine the content of packets transmitted over a network.

5. The correct answer is a. You should delete the message and ignore it. If you click the link and update your details as requested (b), you can wave goodbye to the contents of your bank account. Withdrawing your money and moving it to another bank (c) will have no effect other than annoying your bank manager. Closing your email client and logging off will have no effect at all. The message will still be there the next time you check your email.

INTERNET DEFENCES

- ■ **Social Engineering**
- ■ **Passwords**
- ■ **Email Encryption**
- ■ **Security Suites**
- ■ **Proxy Servers**
- ■ **Back-up/ Restore**
- ■ **Content Filtering**
- ■ **Content Rating**

There are two essential elements to defending yourself on the Internet. The first, and the more important, is to try to **avoid threats** by ensuring that they never reach you. The second is to **remove any threats** that have managed to reach you, although this may happen too late if the damage has already been done.

We have already looked at how you can protect yourself against viruses by installing a good antivirus program and avoid the installation of spyware by using an anti-spyware program. You can also combat spam by using spam-filtering software and use more specialist programs to guard against key loggers and rogue diallers.

Most of these threats come from automated attacks, carried out by computer programs. Other types of attack, possibly even more dangerous, are carried out by malicious individuals. While you may be able to obtain some protection against phishing and pharming by means of security programs, the most effective form of protection is the way you behave online.

SOCIAL ENGINEERING

Many threats can be classed as forms of **social engineering**, the name given to trying to trick people into revealing information. For example, most phishing attacks rely on making the victim feel comfortable by using familiar logos and websites that look and feel like the real thing. Scam emails, like the lottery scam, rely on making victims careless by appealing to their greed. Groomers, lurking in chatrooms, try to befriend young people by pretending that they are the same age as them and that they share their interests.

The solution is to be careful at all times about giving information out online. Remember, once you have posted information about yourself online, it will be out there forever and can potentially be used by almost anyone. Wherever possible, you should try to use a nickname when you are online, use throwaway email addresses and avoid giving out information such as your address or telephone number. If you really need to give out this information, you should send it by email, which is much more secure.

You may have noticed that many websites ask you to supply various items of personal information, so that these can be used as 'security questions' if you forget your password. Typical questions include things like:

- What was the name of the first school you attended?
- What is your boyfriend / girlfriend / partner's name?
- What is your favourite film?
- What is your favourite song?

Take a look at some of your friends' pages on social networking sites such as MySpace or Facebook. Can you find the answers to questions like these? In many cases, criminals no longer even have to guess the answers. They can find out all they want to know about their victims online! The amount of personal information available online has become such a problem that many banks are moving away from using security questions and moving towards greater use of biometric information, such as fingerprints or retinal scans.

 If you use social networking sites, think carefully about what information you want to reveal. Your real friends already know this information. Do you really want to tell everyone else?

 You can find out more about Social Engineering at:
http://www.securityfocus.com/infocus/1527

PASSWORDS

One of the simplest steps you can take to protect your online identity is to use secure **passwords**. A secure password should be at least eight characters long and should contain a mixture of uppercase and lowercase characters, numerals and special characters, such as # or *. Ideally, you should use a different password for each application or service that you use, and you should change your password regularly.

Unfortunately, if you have too many passwords, if they are too long or complex, or if they are changed too often, they become difficult to remember. This usually results in people writing their passwords down, which defeats the purpose of having them.

People often keep a note of their passwords on the underside of their keyboard or mouse pad, making it easy for anyone who has access to their machine to obtain them. In offices, it isn't unusual to see passwords on Post-it notes stuck to the side of a monitor, or to hear someone shouting a request for a password across the room.

 You can find out more about passwords at: http://en.wikipedia.org/wiki/Password

Cracking passwords

Hackers use a variety of techniques to obtain or crack passwords. The simplest one is trying to guess the password. If your password is the name of your boyfriend or girlfriend, your pet or your favourite band, it's going to be relatively easy to guess. Another technique is to try to trick you, or anyone else who knows your password, into revealing it. This is the objective of many phishing attacks.

More sophisticated techniques involve the use of computers to crack passwords. In the past, mainframe computers often took weeks or months to crack a password, but modern PCs are so powerful that they can do this in a relatively short period.

One approach is known as the **dictionary attack**. The computer simply works its way systematically through a dictionary, trying each word in turn, until it finds the correct password. This is why it isn't a good idea to use a real word as your password. Dictionaries exist in languages other than English, so use of a foreign word as a password is no guarantee of security.

One of the most sophisticated forms of attack is known as the **brute-force attack**. The computer simply tries every possible combination of characters until it finds the correct password. It normally starts by trying all possible combinations of two characters, then three characters and so on until it finds the correct combination.

You might think that software for carrying out these types of attack is only available to expert hackers; but anyone who likes can easily buy password-cracking software. A company called **Elcomsoft** sells reasonably priced software which can carry out dictionary or brute-force attacks on a variety of applications. It will even give you an estimate of how long it will take to crack a password.

 You can find out more about cracking passwords at:
http://en.wikipedia.org/wiki/Password_cracking

 Never use a real word as a password, as it can easily be cracked by means of a dictionary attack.

Protecting your passwords

There are various steps you can take to ensure that your passwords are difficult to crack and hard for others to find out:

- **Don't use personal information:** names of family members, friends, pets or simple numbers like your telephone number or date of birth are too easy to guess.
- **Don't use real words:** all real words are too easy to crack by means of dictionary attacks. Hackers often have access to specialist dictionaries, e.g. legal, medical, technical etc. so even obscure words should be avoided.
- **Mix different types of characters:** upper and lower case, numbers and special characters, such as % or @.
- **Use long passwords:** the longer a password is, the harder it is to crack. Passwords should contain a minimum of eight characters.
- **Don't write passwords down:** if you do, someone will find them. You should also be careful that no-one is looking over your shoulder when you enter a password.
- **Use a password manager:** this allows you to store all your passwords in encrypted form in a single location, protected by a single password. This helps you to remember which password is associated with each application. Some password managers can be configured to fill in passwords automatically when you log on to a site.
- **Change passwords regularly:** passwords for online banking etc. should be changed every month or so, while logon passwords should be changed quarterly.
- **Use different passwords for different applications:** if you use the same password all the time, then any hacker who gets hold of it has access to all your applications.
- **Don't enter passwords on public computers:** entering passwords in locations like libraries or Internet cafés is not a good idea, because your data may be stored in the system or intercepted via key loggers. Wireless networks are particularly dangerous unless they are secured.

 You should always choose a password which is at least eight characters long and consists of a mixture of upper and lowercase letters, digits and special characters.

 In the online exam, you could be asked questions about passwords or social engineering. These will be in a similar form to the Test Yourself questions at the end of this chapter.

 You can find out about Steganos Password Manager (and download a free trial) at: https://www.steganos.com/us/products/home-office/password-manager/overview/

 You can view the Elcomsoft range of Password Recovery Software and download limited trial versions at: http://www.elcomsoft.com/

EMAIL ENCRYPTION

One of the simplest ways of protecting your emails from being intercepted and read by hackers or other unauthorised individuals is to use some form of encryption. Most encryption systems depend on the use of two keys: a **public key** and a **private key**.

To send someone a message, you need only know their public key. The recipient can decrypt the message using their private key, known only to them. Similarly, if someone wants to send you a message, they can encrypt it using your public key and you can decrypt it using your private key. Anyone trying to read them without the appropriate key will simply see a string of garbled characters.

One of the best-known email encryption systems is **PGP (Pretty Good Privacy)**. Many email client programs, including Microsoft Outlook, also incorporate encryption features.

You can find out more about PGP and download a copy from:

http://www.pgpi.org/

SECURITY SUITES

We've already looked at various stand-alone products for protecting your computer against Internet threats, e.g. antivirus, anti-spyware and anti-spam software and firewalls. If you want to, you can install all of these products individually, but there is another alternative – installing a **security suite** which protects against a number of threats.

Almost all security software suppliers offer a security suite. Virtually all of these consist of three main components: **antivirus**, **anti-spyware** and a **firewall.** They may or may not offer **anti-spam**, **pop-up blockers** and other additional features. The major advantage of security suites is their **ease of installation**, as you only have to install a single product rather than several different ones. You can also be fairly certain that, as all the components are from the same supplier, they will work well together and there will be **no compatibility problems**.

The biggest drawback is that a suite may contain one top-class product, e.g. the antivirus component, but the other components are of poorer quality. Many experts believe that the anti-spyware component in some security suites is weak, particularly when it comes to removing existing spyware.

We'll take a look now at some of the top security suites and give you some links to others you can check out. Please note that these products are updated continuously, so some details may have changed by the time you check these sites. Most of the producers are happy to allow you to download a time-limited trial version of their software. After a month or so, you need to pay for a subscription if you want the software kept up to date.

Norton Internet Security

The Norton Internet Security suite (from Symantec) offers antivirus, anti-spyware, a two-way firewall, advanced phishing protection, intrusion prevention and rootkit detection. Anti-spam and parental protection features are available as an add-on.

According to the producers, the suite:
- Removes viruses and Internet worms automatically
- Protects email and instant messaging from viruses
- Protects against hackers
- Blocks identity theft by phishing websites.

 You can obtain further information and download a trial copy from: http://www.symantec.com/norton/products/overview.jsp?pcid=is&pvid=nis2008

McAfee Internet Security Suite

The McAfee Internet Security Suite is a comprehensive package which includes antivirus, anti-spyware, firewall, anti-spam and anti-phishing, privacy and identity-theft protection, parental controls and file back-up and restore.
According to the producers, the McAfee Internet Security Suite:
- Provides online security from identity thieves, spammers and predators
- Protects your PC from viruses, hackers and spyware
- Backs up and restores your photos, music and important files
- Protects your online experience so you can surf the web, shop, bank, email and instant message safely and securely

- Intercepts prohibited websites, unwanted activity and offensive pictures to keep your family safe
- Warns you about sites which send spam, install adware or attempt online scams.

 You can obtain further information and download a trial copy from: http://www.uk.mcafee.com

Panda Internet Security Suite

The Panda Internet Security Suite is a comprehensive package which includes antivirus, anti-spyware, anti-phishing, firewall, identity protection, back-up, anti-spam and parental control.

According to the producers, the suite uses a new and exclusive security model that guarantees detection of more than a million viruses and other threats, offering levels of protection far higher than traditional antiviruses.

 In the online exam, you could be asked questions about security suites. These will be in a similar form to the Test Yourself questions at the end of this chapter.

 Now would be a good time to complete the section of your log book relating to security suites. You might want to install and configure an Internet security suite or compare different Internet security suites. Your tutor should be able to advise you further.

 You can obtain further information and download a trial copy from: http://www.pandasecurity.com/homeusers/solutions/internet-security/

Many other online security companies produce Internet security suites. Some of the major ones are listed below:

Kaspersky: http://www.kaspersky.com/kaspersky_internet_security

Steganos: https://www.steganos.com/us/products/home-office/security-suite/overview/

Bullguard: http://www.bullguard.com/why/bullguard-internet-security.aspx

Trend Micro: http://us.trendmicro.com/us/products/personal/trend-micro-internet-security-2007/

PROXY SERVERS

Whenever you communicate with a server on the Internet, e.g. Google or MySpace, you pass over several items of information that could potentially be used by hackers. One of the most important of these is your **IP address**, which can be used to identify your computer, or even you personally.

The information passed to external sites may depend on how your PC is connected to the Internet, e.g. via direct dial-up or ADSL at home or via a Local Area Network (LAN) at school or at work. It may also depend on the IP address-allocation policy of your Internet Service Provider (ISP). The revealed IP address might be one that can be traced to your own machine or one that can only be traced back as far as your ISP.

Many users believe that it is unwise to reveal such data to external sites, as it poses a possible security risk. Others simply insist that they have a right to surf without being traced. One solution is to surf via a **proxy server**.

A proxy server sits between your computer and the websites it accesses. It strips the IP address from any message you transmit and replaces it with a fake IP address, meaning that sites which you access are unable to see your real IP address. Many proxy server products make use of Secure Socket Layer (SSL) technology, as used by banks to secure online transactions.

One such product is **Anonymous Surfing** from Anonymizer, which redirects your web traffic through secure servers. It also protects you against visiting known phishing, pharming or spyware sites, by displaying a warning message if you try to do so. One unusual feature of Anonymous Surfing is protection against **Evil Twins.** These are rogue wireless hotspots that try to trick users into connecting a laptop or PDA to them by posing as a legitimate wireless provider. If you connect to their wireless network, the evil twins can see everything you transmit and steal confidential information such as account numbers and passwords.

Identity Protection:	
Anonymous Surfing keeps your IP address and your online identity secure.	
Real IP Address	212.███.██.██
Everyone else sees	**198.172.201.70**

Steganos offers a number of products for concealing your IP address, including **Internet Anonym** which establishes a **Virtual Private Network (VPN)** tunnel between your computer and one of their servers. All your Internet activities are then carried via that tunnel, which encrypts all information passing through it by using an SSL connection. This protects the information from being eavesdropped on – even by your ISP. Any websites that you visit only see the IP

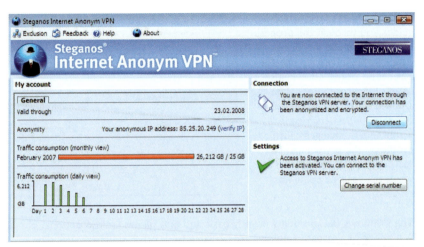

address of the Steganos servers. The price of Internet Anonym depends on the amount of traffic you transmit and receive. It costs around £50 per year for 25 GB per month (far more than most users will need) or around £200 per year for unlimited traffic.

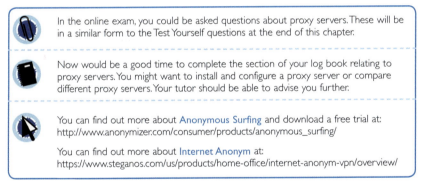

In the online exam, you could be asked questions about proxy servers. These will be in a similar form to the Test Yourself questions at the end of this chapter.

Now would be a good time to complete the section of your log book relating to proxy servers. You might want to install and configure a proxy server or compare different proxy servers. Your tutor should be able to advise you further.

You can find out more about Anonymous Surfing and download a free trial at: http://www.anonymizer.com/consumer/products/anonymous_surfing/

You can find out more about Internet Anonym at: https://www.steganos.com/us/products/home-office/internet-anonym-vpn/overview/

BACK-UP/RESTORE

One of the most important steps you can take to safeguard your data is making regular back-ups. Windows XP includes a basic Backup utility (ntbackup) which allows you to back up and restore files, folders and other system data. This can be done manually or scheduled to take place automatically. The utility supports all kinds of storage devices and media, including tape drives, removable disks and recordable CD-ROMs and DVDs.

The Backup utility is normally started by selecting **Start > All Programs > Accessories > System Tools** and clicking **Backup**. This starts the **Backup**

or Restore Wizard, which guides you through the process of backing up and restoring data. Making a back-up creates a **restore point**, i.e. a snapshot of all of the computer's data and the state of the operating system at a particular time. If subsequent changes cause problems, the system can be restored to the state it was in when the restore point was created.

The Windows Backup utility is fairly basic and only allows limited options. A number of alternative utilities are available from other suppliers, including **Acronis True Image Home** which allows you to create an exact copy of your PC for a full back-up or back up only your important data and application settings. It allows a wide range of storage devices to be used for back-up, and you can recover your entire system, an important file or your application settings.

Online back-ups

Another alternative is to back up your critical data to an online back-up site. You can do this yourself by copying files manually to online hosting sites like **MegaUpload**, which offers 50 GB of free storage and excellent File Manager software. **RapidShare** and **GigaSize** are other sites which offer similar facilities. These sites only normally store files for a fixed length of time, e.g. ninety days in the case of MegaUpload, but this may not be important if you are using them for regular back-ups.

You may find it more convenient to use an online back-up service like **MozyHome**, a simple and effective system which allows you to create online back-ups easily. A free version is available, allowing up to 2 GB of data to be backed up.

You simply create a user account which will allow you to download and install the MozyHome software. After that, you check the boxes for the types of files you want to back up, and MozyHome does the rest. You can also select specific files and directories.

MozyHome will back up your documents whether they're open or closed and allows documents to be **encrypted**. MozyHome finds and saves the smallest changes, and you can schedule the times to make back-ups. After the initial back-up, MozyHome only backs up files that have been added or changed, making subsequent back-ups extremely rapid.

You can find out more about Acronis True Image, and download an evaluation, copy at: http://www.acronis.com/

You can find out about MozyHome and sign up for a free account at: http://mozy.com/home

You can check out the following online hosting sites, all of which offer free storage options:

RapidShare: http://rapidshare.com/

MegaUpload: http://www.megaupload.com/signup/

GigaSize: http://www.gigasize.com/

CONTENT FILTERING

Content-filtering software attempts to block or allow access to websites depending on their content. Its main purpose is to avoid having young people exposed to Internet pornography, but it can also block other undesirable sites, including those with terrorist, racist or violent content. Content-filtering software is mainly used by parents to control content, block websites and set up passwords. Some products offer additional features like email filtering, pop-up blocking and chatroom monitoring. Many products also offer logging of online activities.

Good content-filtering software should offer a good balance between filtering objectionable material and not filtering too much content. Content-filtering programs use a range of different techniques, including URL filtering, keyword filtering and dynamic filtering.

- **URL filtering** involves maintaining lists of URLs which have been judged acceptable (whitelists) or unacceptable (blacklists). Unfortunately, there are grey areas, for example, many states in the USA are opposed to the teaching of the Theory of Evolution, so should sites discussing this be blocked? The most effective URL filters are those which are closely monitored by human observers, but this is expensive and time-consuming. Some filtering software allows parents to add URLs to whitelists or blacklists.
- **Keyword filtering** depends on blocking sites because of the existence of particular keywords. Unfortunately, this tends to result in blocking sites which have nothing wrong with them. This is sometimes referred to as 'overblocking'. For example, blocking sites by using a list of sexual keywords may lead to the blocking of sites giving advice on AIDS, breast cancer etc.
- **Dynamic filtering** analyses the content of a web page each time an attempt is made to access it. The page is then allowed or blocked on the basis of the content encountered. This is much more useful than URL filtering, since it works with any website, but it can suffer from the same problems as keyword filtering.

There are other approaches to filtering. Researchers at Macquarie University in Australia discovered that 40 per cent of pornographic web pages included more than five links to images or movies, compared to just 0.8 per cent of other pages, and that normal pages have almost twice as many words on average (662 compared to 388) than pornographic pages. By applying a statistical technique known as Bayesian analysis, they were able to produce a filter that accurately predicted a website as being pornographic or not in 99.1 per cent of cases, well above the 87 per cent accuracy of most commercial systems.

 Content-filtering software can be a useful method of blocking undesirable content, but it can also block harmless content inadvertently.

There are a number of commercial content-filtering programs available. We will look briefly at three of the most popular.

Net Nanny

Net Nanny is probably the most popular content-filtering program available at present. It uses a technique called **Dynamic Contextual Analysis** to filter web content. For example, a news site could be blocked early in the day due to a particularly violent story, but if the content changes later in the day the site would be allowed again. Net Nanny also offers the facility of warning about potentially objectionable material and letting the user decide whether to proceed or not. Another useful feature is the ability to override blocked websites by entering a password.

Net Nanny has a good reputation for avoiding both overblocking and underblocking (letting unacceptable sites through). It is also good at detecting objectionable sites in languages other than English. It includes remote management and reporting functions which allow parents to view activity logs and make configuration changes from anywhere in the world and can notify parents instantly via email if children attempt to access objectionable material.

Net Nanny allows parents to see and control every site in its database. It can be configured to filter out negative sites or only allow access to positive sites and can prevent personal information, such as names, addresses, phone numbers, email addresses, credit card numbers etc. from being given out over the Internet. If a child tries to reveal these details in an email or instant message, the software replaces it with a row of Xs. Net Nanny's activity log tracks the websites, newsgroups and chatrooms that children visit and the information they send and receive.

 You can find out more about **Net Nanny** and download a time-limited trial version at: http://www.netnanny.com/

CYBERsitter

CYBERsitter is designed for home, educational or small-business use. Like most other filtering products, it can block access to undesirable websites and record details of all websites visited. Filtering is generally effective and avoids overblocking or underblocking. It can also record both sides of chat conversations and offers a social networking category that can block services like MySpace and Facebook. Parents can set time restrictions on Internet usage and receive monitoring reports by email. CYBERsitter offers a number of unique features including email filtering and the ability to scan your hard drive for objectionable material.

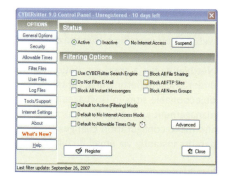

You can find out more about CYBERsitter and download a time-limited trial version at: http://www.cybersitter.com/

CyberPatrol

CyberPatrol is a powerful and popular client-based, browser independent, content-filtering program for Windows-based stand-alone PCs. It can be used to monitor Internet activity, block undesirable sites and images, restrict chat and instant messaging, limit time online and access to programs and control program downloads. It can also help protect privacy by preventing private information, like names/addresses/ phone numbers, from being revealed and by setting up rules so that confidential information is filtered out before it leaves your computer.

You can find out more about CyberPatrol and download a time-limited trial version at: http://www.cyberpatrol.com/

Content filtering for business

There are a number of sophisticated content-filtering systems, sometimes described as Web Filtering Appliances, available for use by businesses who wish to protect their networks and control employee access to the Internet. These systems can be used to prevent employees from downloading undesirable content and ensure that time is not wasted surfing non-business-related sites during working hours.

The **Barracuda Web Filter** uses a combination of hardware and software to provide an integrated content-filtering, application-blocking and spyware-protection system. It blocks access to websites based on URL or content category, blocks downloads based on file type and blocks applications that access the Internet, including instant messaging and music services. A similar product is available from **Content Watch**, the suppliers of Net Nanny.

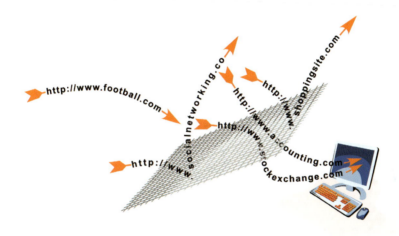

You can find out more about the Barracuda Web Filter at:
http://www.barracudanetworks.com/ns/products/spyware_overview.php

You can find out more about Net Nanny and download a time-limited trial version at: http://www.netnanny.com/

You can find out more about CYBERsitter and download a time-limited trial version at: http://www.cybersitter.com/

You can find out more about CyberPatrol and download a time-limited trial version at: http://www.cyberpatrol.com/

CONTENT RATING

The **Internet Content Rating Association (ICRA)** has developed a content-description system which allows web masters and content creators to label their content in categories such as nudity, sex, language, violence and other potentially harmful material. The IRCA system is based on the **Platform for Internet Content Selection (PICS)** specification, which enables labels to be associated with Internet content. It was originally designed by the World Wide Web Consortium (W3C) to help parents and teachers control what children access on the Internet.

IRCA does not itself label content; it only provides the opportunity for content providers to do so by completing a web-based questionnaire. The system relies to some extent on providers labelling their content accurately, but IRCA does offer a content-validation service.

Most of the filtering software which we looked at earlier supports the ICRA content-rating system; and many web browsers, such as **Internet Explorer**, support it directly. You can configure the content settings by selecting **Internet Options** in Internet Explorer's **Tools** menu.

Content Rating only works if content providers rate their content and your browser is configured to support it.

You can find out more about the Internet Content Rating Association (ICRA) at: http://www.fosi.org/icra/

You can find out more about the Platform for Internet Content Selection (PICS) at: http://www.w3.org/PICS/

You can find out how to use and configure the Internet Explorer Content Advisor at: http://www.microsoft.com/technet/prodtechnol/ie/reskit/6/part2/c05ie6rkmspx?mfr=true

In the online exam, you could be asked questions about content filtering and content rating. These will be in a similar form to the Test Yourself questions at the end of this chapter.

Now would be a good time to complete the section of your log book relating to content filtering. You might want to install and configure content-filtering software or compare different content-filtering products. The log should also give details of the steps you have taken to generate secure passwords and back up and restore critical files. It should not contain examples of genuine passwords. Your tutor should be able to advise you further.

TEST YOURSELF

1. **What is the name given to techniques which involve trying to trick computer users into parting with confidential information?**
   a. Social engineering.
   b. Social networking.
   c. Social climbing.
   d. Social science.

2. **Which of the following would be the best password?**
   a. Rover.
   b. PartickThistle.
   c. JmQ@#123b.
   d. 10December.

3. **You open an email message from a friend and you see something like the following:**

   mQGiBD8VvQcRBADC5xKkPd9CN0Lp5ojkF//
   fquj3ak8VDljlf0SK/ZeOKBFHWI/O
   IGB4yrvvz8kx+OZBygykxh5emQs4Bw8EO0oxoFYC9MyNw5j
   OAKaLaxyv6UzkD7xW

   What is the most likely reason for this?
   a. The message has been corrupted during transmission.
   b. Your friend has a faulty keyboard.
   c. The message is encrypted.
   d. Your friend is learning Klingon.

4. **What is the name given to a system which prevents your true IP address from being revealed to websites?**
   a. Domain name server.
   b. Proxy server.
   c. Process server.
   d. File server.

5. **What type of software prevents objectionable material from being displayed on your screen?**
   a. Antivirus software.
   b. Spam-filtering software.
   c. Content-filtering software.
   d. Anti-spyware software.

ANSWERS

1. The correct answer is a. The name given to techniques which involve trying to trick computer users into parting with confidential information is social engineering. Social networking (b) involves using software for communication and collaboration. Social climbing (c) is trying to rise up through the social hierarchy. Social science (d) is the group of sciences which includes Psychology, Sociology and Economics.

2. The correct answer is c. JmQ@#123b would be the best password, as it is nine characters long and uses uppercase, lowercase, numeric and special characters. Rover (a) would not be a good choice, as it's probably the name of your pet and easy to find out. Similarly, PartickThistle (b) is not a good choice, as it's fairly easy for someone to find out who your favourite football team is. 10 December (d) is not a good choice, as when people use dates as passwords they normally pick significant ones like birthdays.

3. The correct answer is c. The message has probably been encrypted. If the message had been corrupted during transmission (a), it probably wouldn't open at all. If your friend had a faulty keyboard (b), she'd probably notice that the message was garbage before sending it. The text shown doesn't look anything like Klingon (d)!

4. The correct answer is b. A system which prevents your true IP address from being revealed to websites is called a proxy server. A domain name server (a) issues IP addresses to computers on a Local Area Network. Process server (c) is a legal term which has no meaning in computing. A file server (d) is a system which stores files on a computer network.

5. The correct answer is c. Content-filtering software prevents objectionable material from being displayed on your screen. Antivirus software (a) prevents viruses from infecting your machine. Spam-filtering software (b)prevents spam emails from being displayed, and anti-spyware software (d)prevents spyware from being installed on your machine.

THE INTERNET AND THE LAW

- **Copyright**
- **Downloading Files**
- **Digital Rights Management**
- **Disability Discrimination Act**
- **Data Protection Act 1998**
- **Other Relevant Laws**
- **Online Behaviour**

Whenever you are using the Internet, you should bear in mind that there are a number of legal considerations you need to be aware of. In particular:

- If you are downloading files, you should be aware of the fact that these may be subject to copyright restrictions.
- If you are producing websites, you should take care to ensure that they are accessible to users with disabilities.
- If you are storing data online, you should be aware of the provisions of the Data Protection Act.
- You should also know that your online behaviour, particularly what you say to or about people, is subject to the same legal restrictions as real-world behaviour.

COPYRIGHT

Copyright refers to the right of the creators of literary, dramatic, musical and artistic works to control how their works are used. This includes control of broadcast and public performance, copying, adapting, issuing, renting and lending copies. Copyright applies to any original work which exhibits a degree of labour, skill or judgement. It does not apply to ideas, only to products. If a work is produced as part of employment, copyright normally belongs to the employer rather than the employee who created the work. Most copyright in the UK is covered by the **Copyright, Designs and Patents Act 1988 (CDPA)**. The **Copyright (Computer Programs) Regulations 1992** extended the rules covering literary works to include computer programs. Copyrights, designs, patents and trademarks are sometimes referred to as **'intellectual property'**.

Copyright is automatic. There is no need for the producer of a work to register it as copyright, but they may find it easier to prove their ownership of the work if they do so. There are some exemptions from copyright, based on the principle of 'fair use'. This normally allows the making of limited extracts from copyright materials for the purposes of review or criticism, or for educational use. There are also exemptions for 'incidental use', for example if you make a home movie which has a copyrighted song playing on the radio in the background.

Duration of copyright

The duration of copyright can vary depending on the type of work:

- For **literary, dramatic, musical or artistic works**, copyright normally lasts for seventy years from the end of the calendar year in which the last remaining author dies, or the work is made available to the public by authorised performance, broadcast, exhibition etc.
- For **sound recordings** and broadcasts, copyright normally lasts for fifty years from the end of the calendar year in which the last remaining author of the work dies, or the work is made available to the public by authorised release, performance, broadcast etc.
- For **films**, copyright normally lasts for seventy years from the end of the calendar year in which the last principal director, author or composer dies, or the work is made available to the public by authorised performance, broadcast, exhibition etc.

Copyright and the Internet

It's a common misconception that anything available on the Internet is 'public domain' or free of copyright. This is simply untrue. The vast majority of material published on the Internet is subject to exactly the same copyright restrictions as material published in other media. This applies to text, photographs, videos, music and other types of media. Material is only public-domain if its period of copyright has expired or if the copyright owner has explicitly placed it in the public domain.

There are some notable exceptions, such as Wikipedia, the free encyclopedia. All of the text in Wikipedia, and most of the other content, is covered by the **GNU Free Documentation Licence (GFDL)**. Wikipedia articles (and there are over 2 million of them in English alone) remain the property of their creators, but the GFDL allows the content to be reproduced, with certain restrictions.

Despite the name, the GFDL can be applied to any type of content, including music, images, video and software. It is not restricted to documents. Another similar licence, the **Creative Commons** licence, can also be applied to all types of media.

It is normally regarded as acceptable to insert **hyperlinks** to a website within an online document. Hyperlinks should normally be to the home page of a website, or a page high in the hierarchy. **Hotlinking** to individual images is discouraged and is often regarded as a form of bandwidth theft.

Don't assume that anything you find on the internet is free of copyright. In most instances, this won't be the case.

You can find a useful summary of UK copyright legislation at: http://copyrightservice.co.uk/copyright/uk_law_summary

You can read the complete text of the Copyright, Designs and Patents Act 1988 at: http://www.opsi.gov.uk/acts/acts1988/Ukpga_19880048_en_1.htm

You can read 10 Common Copyright Myths at: http://www.copyrightservice.co.uk/copyright/copyright_myths

You can read an interesting UK Government paper on Copyright and the Internet at: http://www.parliament.uk/post/pn185.pdf

DOWNLOADING FILES

You should never download files from the Internet using file-sharing systems such as Kazaa or Limewire. As already noted, many of the files available, including films, music and software, are copyright, so downloading them is illegal. There is also a moral issue: the producers of these works are entitled to income from them, and illegal downloading deprives them of this.

Downloads are often incomplete or of poor quality, for example, films recorded by taking a video camera into a cinema, or highly compressed digital music. However, there is another, and perhaps stronger, reason for not downloading files. Many downloaded files contain viruses or spyware, for example, video files which ask you to 'acquire a licence' to play them and then download malware when you attempt to do so. Some of the software used for file sharing, most notably Kazaa, is known to be bundled with spyware.

It can be dangerous to have a file-sharing folder open on your computer, as any user of the same file-sharing system can see what files you have in it and can download them from your system. Some file-sharing programs allow the file-sharing folder to be disabled, but with others, such as BitTorrent clients, it is an integral part of the file-sharing system and cannot be disabled.

Music-industry organisations, like the Recording Industry Association of America (RIAA), have actively prosecuted major uploaders of shared files, but they are also believed to have attempted prosecution of around 20 000 individual users who have only downloaded files. Other organisations, such as the Electronic Frontier Foundation (EFF), believe that RIAA has been a bit heavy-handed, and support an approach which permits file sharing but allows copyright holders to receive payment.

A major file-sharing site, Demonoid.com was recently forced to close when the Canadian Recording Industry association (CRIA) threatened their ISP with legal action.

Other organisations, including the **Federation Against Software Theft (FAST)** and the **Business Software Alliance (BSA)**, investigate software piracy and take action against offenders.

Legal downloads

Although it is illegal to download pirated copies of commercial software, it is perfectly legal to download various other types of software, for example:

- **Freeware:** software which is completely free.
- **Shareware:** software which you can 'try before you buy'. Shareware programs often have restrictions, such as placing an image on every page produced or only running a certain number of times.
- **Demo versions:** major software producers often allow demo versions of their programs to be downloaded and run for a limited period. If you wish to continue running the software after this period has elapsed, you must buy a copy.
- **Open source:** again, this is completely free. In this case, the source code (i.e. the original computer programs, in a language like C or Java) are also made available to anyone who wants to amend them. Well-known open source programs include the **Linux** operating system, the **Apache** web server and the **Open Office** business applications suite.

There are also a number of sites where you can download music legally, either paying by the track or for a whole album. These include **iTunes**, **Napster** and even **Tesco**! Other sites allow you to download free music, often from up-and-coming bands. These include **music.download.com** and **mp3.com**.

Don't download copyrighted files. You risk prosecution as well as exposing your computer to viruses and other dangers.

 In the online exam, you could be asked questions about copyright or related topics. These will be in a similar form to the Test Yourself questions at the end of this chapter.

 Now would be a good time to complete the section of your log book relating to downloading files. You might want to give examples of downloading music or video from legal sites or research sites (free and pay) where music/video can be downloaded legally. Your tutor should be able to advise you further.

 You can read the RIAA's views on music downloads at: http://www.riaa.com/physicalpiracy.php?content_selector=piracy_details_online and the EFF's opposing views at: http://www.eff.org/share/

You can visit the FAST website at: http://www.fast.org.uk/ and the BSA site at: http://www.bsa.org

You can find out about the GNU Free Documentation Licence at: http://en.wikipedia.org/wiki/GNU_Free_Documentation_License

Music download links include:
iTunes: http://www.apple.com/itunes/overview/
Napster: http://www.napstersongs.co.uk
Tesco: http://www.tescodownloads.com
Music Download: http://music.download.com/
MP3: http://www.mp3.com
Software download links include:
Download.com: http://www.download.com/
Tucows: http://www.tucows.com/

DIGITAL RIGHTS MANAGEMENT

Content producers, such as record companies and movie studios, have always objected to attempts to copy their products, even before the introduction of digital technologies. Record companies objected to the copying of music on to tape, and movie studies objected to films being copied on to video tape.

However, the problem has become much more widespread since the introduction of digital technologies. Content has become much more easily available, and copying has become much easier: even a very basic computer can copy CDs and DVDs. Unlike the situation with analogue technologies, there is no deterioration in quality as products are copied – a tenth-generation copy sounds every bit as good as a first-generation copy. Illegal copying of CDs, DVDs and software is sometimes referred to as **digital piracy**.

Digital Rights Management (DRM) tries to control the ways in which digital products can be used, copied or converted to other formats. Some critics claim that DRM allows copyright holders too much control, as it can prevent or impede legal uses of products as well as illegal ones. For example, some DRM mechanisms will not permit CDs or DVDs to be played on a computer, although the buyer has a right to play them on any device. Critics claim that DRM should be more accurately described as Digital Restrictions Management.

There have been various attempts to use DRM schemes on music CDs, including the notorious Sony rootkit scandal, which we discussed earlier. These have not been particularly successful, and no major record company is currently selling CDs with DRM protection. Many online music stores, most notably Apple's **iTunes**, have adopted DRM, but others, such as **eMusic** and **Musicload.de**, have resisted it as it is unpopular with buyers, partly because it ties users to specific companies or products. It is also confusing to users because a number of different systems are in use. The number of times you can copy a track, or transfer it to another system, depends largely on where you obtained it and the DRM techniques used.

If you buy digitally protected music, there will be restrictions on how often you can copy it and what devices it can be played on.

The US **Digital Millennium Copyright Act (DMCA)** makes it a criminal offence to produce or distribute technology that allows users to get round copy-protection schemes. The EU **Copyright Directive** issued in 2001 contains similar provisions. These laws have been heavily criticised, with some critics claiming that they are inhibiting legitimate research in areas such as cryptography because the work could be applied in breaking copy-protection schemes.

DRM has not been particularly successful as a method of preventing copying, as all of the schemes used to date have quickly been cracked. All methods of protecting audio content suffer from a problem known as the 'analogue hole'. Any type of digital audio has to be converted back to analogue form in order to hear it. While it is in analogue form it can be recorded, and the analogue recordings can then be converted back to an unprotected digital format.

You can find out more about Digital Rights Management (DRM) at: http://news.bbc.co.uk/2/hi/technology/6337781.stm

You can read criticisms of DRM at: http://drm.info/

Digital watermarking

Digital watermarking is used to protect graphical images by marking them in such a way that their source can be identified. Watermarks may be visible or invisible. Companies which supply stock photographs via the Internet often place a visible watermark (such as the company name and a copyright symbol) on the images displayed on their websites, so that these cannot simply be downloaded and used instead of buying an image.

Museums and art galleries may also place visible watermarks on images of items from their collections to indicate the source of the image.

The BBC has started watermarking images from 'Doctor Who' on its website because they were being used to produce pirate merchandise.

It is now becoming increasingly common for the owners of images to use **invisible watermarks** to identify the images and their source. These make use of a technique known as **steganography**, originally designed to allow coded messages to be hidden within pictures.

Even a fairly small digital image contains a large number of bits: for example, a 640 x 480-pixel image in 24-bit colour contains nearly 60 million bits. The simplest watermarking techniques involve changing a fairly small number of bits in order to hide a message. This makes no visible difference to the image.

Digital fingerprints are unique labels inserted into different copies of the same content (e.g. an e-book, video or music file) prior to distribution. Each digital fingerprint is associated with a single copy, allowing content owners to trace buyers who use their content for unintended purposes. Fingerprints are closely associated with the content and are difficult to remove.

You can read more about digital watermarks at:
http://www.webreference.com/content/watermarks/

You can download a trial copy of The Watermark Factory from:
http://www.watermarkfactory.com/

You can check out the BBC's watermarked Doctor Who images at:
http://www.bbc.co.uk/doctorwho/gallery/

DISABILITY DISCRIMINATION ACT

If you produce websites, you must comply with the Disability Discrimination Act (DDA), which aims to ensure that websites are accessible to blind and disabled users. Although there is no mention of web accessibility in the Act itself, there are several mentions in the associated Code of Practice, which makes the following points which are relevant to websites:

The Disability Discrimination Act makes it unlawful for a service provider to discriminate against a disabled person by refusing to provide any service which it provides to members of the public.

From 1 October 1999, a service provider has to take reasonable steps to change a practice which makes it unreasonably difficult for disabled people to make use of its services.

What services are affected by the Disability Discrimination Act? An airline company provides a flight-reservation and booking service to the public on its website. This is a provision of a service and is subject to the Act.

For people with visual impairments, the range of auxiliary aids or services which it might be reasonable to provide to ensure that services are accessible might include ... accessible websites.

For people with hearing disabilities, the range of auxiliary aids or services which it might be reasonable to provide to ensure that services are accessible might include ... accessible websites.

If your website makes it impossible or unreasonably difficult to access information and services, a disabled person can make a claim against you. If you have not made reasonable adjustments and cannot show that this failure is justified, then you may have to pay compensation and be ordered by a court to change your site.

In a case brought against the Sydney Olympics Committee in Australia in 2000, the court ruled against the website owners, requiring them to pay $20 000 Australian.

 If you produce web-sites, you must ensure that they are accessible to users with disabilities, e.g. those using screen reader software.

DATA PROTECTION ACT 1998

If you store information about individuals on a computer, you must comply with the Data Protection Act 1998, which gives individuals the right to know what information is held about them and tries to ensure that personal information is handled properly. Personal data processed by an individual only for the purposes of personal, family or household affairs is exempted. The operation of the Act is supervised by the Information Commissioner's Office, a public body which promotes access to official information and protects personal information.

The Act states that anyone who processes data must adhere to eight principles:

- Data must be fairly and lawfully processed.
- Data must be processed for limited purposes.
- Data must be adequate, relevant and not excessive.
- Data must be accurate and up to date.
- Data must not be kept for longer than is necessary.
- Data must be processed in line with your rights.
- Data must be stored securely.
- Data must not be transferred to other countries without adequate protection.

The Act also gives individuals the right to find out what information is held about them on computer and on most paper records. If an individual or organisation believes that they are being denied access to information they are entitled to, or feels that their information has not been handled according to the eight principles, they can complain to the Information Commissioner's Office.

 The Data Protection Act places restrictions on what data can be stored about individuals and how it can be used. It also gives users the right to see data held about them.

 You can find a useful summary of the Data Protection Act at:
http://www.jisclegal.ac.uk/dataprotection/dataprotection.htm

You can read the Data Protection Act itself at:
http://www.opsi.gov.uk/acts/acts1998/19980029.htm

You can find out more about the work of the Information Commissioner's Office at:
http://www.ico.gov.uk/

OTHER RELEVANT LAWS

There are other laws which determine what is or is not permissible online. The most important ones include:

- **The Terrorism Act (2006):** makes it illegal to promote or glorify terrorism in any manner, including the use of websites.
- **The Computer Misuse Act (1990):** makes it illegal to use a computer system without the explicit permission of the owner. This would include hacking into a system, looking at files on a computer or using it to access the Internet.
- **The Communications Act (2003):** makes it illegal to obtain Internet access dishonestly, e.g. by logging in on an unsecured wireless connection. This is also an offence under the Computer Misuse Act.
- **The Regulation of Investigatory Powers Act (2000):** gives many government agencies the right to monitor email and to demand the keys to encrypted data. In most cases, a court order or the permission of the Home

Secretary is required to exercise these powers. Many critics believe that the Act represents a serious threat to civil liberties, especially as the European Convention on Human Rights states that *'Everyone has the right to respect for his private and family life, his home and his correspondence' (Article 8(1)).*

- **The Race Relations Act (1976):** prohibits the publication of racist material. This includes racist material on websites.

There is a wide range of legal restrictions on what you can or cannot do on the Internet.

You can find out more about the Terrorism Act and related legislation at: http://www.homeoffice.gov.uk/security/terrorism-and-the-law/

You can find out more about the Computer Misuse Act at: http://en.wikipedia.org/wiki/Computer_Misuse_Act

You can read about an arrest under the Communications Act at: http://news.bbc.co.uk/2/hi/uk_news/england/london/6958429.stm

You can read some of the criticisms of the Regulation of Investigatory Powers Act at: http://en.wikipedia.org/wiki/Regulation_of_Investigatory_Powers_Act_2000

ONLINE BEHAVIOUR

We've already highlighted the importance of behaving correctly online when we were talking about identity theft, but there are other areas you need to consider. Once you say anything online, whether by posting it on a blog, discussing it in a newsgroup or sending it in an email message, you should assume that it will be there forever.

The first email message was sent in 1971, and it's still around. Many other email messages are still stored on individual machines or on mail servers throughout the world. Newsgroup postings have been archived since the earliest days of Usenet, and old versions of websites can be found on Internet archives like the Wayback Machine. It may seem like a great joke when you're setting up your Facebook or MySpace site today, but do you really want future employers looking at it in ten years' time?

One of the most important rules is to behave as carefully online as you would offline. If something you say is likely to lead to legal consequences offline, it is equally likely to do so online. The penalties can be severe, as can be seen from the following stories:

- Neal Patterson, Chief Executive of Cerner, a major IT company in the healthcare sector, sent a terse email message about decline in the company's work ethic to a group of senior managers. Unfortunately, the message was distributed much more widely than intended and was eventually published outwith the company. Investors interpreted it as a sign that the company was in trouble, leading to a 29 per cent drop in the value of its shares.

- Edinburgh bookseller Joe Gordon was sacked by the company he worked for because he occasionally mentioned bad days at work and made fun of his boss in his blog. He was accused of 'gross misconduct' and 'bringing the company into disrepute'.
- Agnes Wilkie, a television producer with Scottish Television (STV), was sacked from her job as head of features for sending insulting emails about her boss to his personal assistant. An Employment Tribunal later ruled that she had been unfairly dismissed, but she was not reinstated.

Unfair or inaccurate online comments about other people can have serious legal consequences.

You can look at older versions of websites on the Wayback Machine at: http://www.archive.org/index.php

Acceptable Use Policies

Many places where computer and Internet access is available, including virtually all schools, colleges and libraries, have an **Acceptable Use Policy (AUP)**. AUPs can vary according to local circumstances, but each person using computer facilities is normally required to indicate acceptance of the policy. Try to obtain a copy of the AUP for your own school, college or library.

AUPs normally state that Internet access is monitored by manual and electronic means and that records of Internet access are kept. The AUP should also specify the actions and penalties which could result from breaching these conditions. These can include passing information to the police if it is suspected that a criminal act has taken place.

You can find out more about Acceptable Use Policies at: http://www.media-awareness.ca/english/resources/special_initiatives/wa_resources/wa_teachers/backgrounders/acceptable_use.cfm

Netiquette

A number of individuals and organisations have suggested that a set of rules should be established for online behaviour. Although there are variations between the different suggested sets of rules, there tends to be a common core. One of the best-known sets of rules is that proposed by Virginia Shea in her book entitled *Netiquette*:

- Remember the Human
- Adhere to the same standards of behaviour online that you follow in real life
- Know where you are in cyberspace

- Respect other people's time and bandwidth
- Make yourself look good online
- Share expert knowledge
- Help keep flame wars under control
- Respect other people's privacy
- Don't abuse your power
- Be forgiving of other people's mistakes.

There are a number of other aspects of netiquette that you should be aware of. You should never write email, newsgroup or chatroom messages entirely in capitals, as this is regarded as equivalent to shouting. Several shorthand techniques have been developed for writing messages. These include the use of **abbreviations** such as LOL ('laughing out loud') and YMMV ('your mileage may vary' – meaning 'your experience may differ').

Small graphics known as **emoticons** or **smileys** are often included in messages. The original emoticons were simple combinations of keyboard characters, such as :) for 'smile' or :(for 'frown', but they have since become much more elaborate, as shown in the following screenshot of emoticons used in Microsoft Live Messenger.

One word of warning – be careful if you receive a pop-up message or an email offering to let you download free smileys. Offers like this are often used to entice people into downloading viruses or spyware.

 In the online exam, you could be asked questions on any of the topics covered in this chapter. These will be in a similar form to the Test Yourself questions at the end of this chapter.

 Now would be a good time to complete the section of your log book relating to online behaviour. You might want to research, compare or construct Acceptable Use Policies or construct checklists for user behaviour or list techniques for withholding personal information (throwaway email addresses, restricting access to personal homepages, anonymiser software etc.). Your tutor should be able to advise you further.

TEST YOURSELF

1. How long does copyright on sound recordings last for?

   a. 25 years.
   b. 50 years.
   c. 70 years.
   d. 100 years.

2. What does DRM stand for?

   a. Digitally Recorded Music.
   b. Digitally Recorded Movie.
   c. Digital Rights Management.
   d. Digital Relay Mixer.

3. What is the name given to the technique of hiding a message or a fingerprint in a graphics file?

   a. Steganography.
   b. Stenography.
   c. Spectroscopy.
   d. Speleology.

4. Which Act gives government agencies the right to monitor email?

   a. Computer Misuse Act.
   b. Communications Act.
   c. Regulation of Investigatory Powers Act.
   d. Data Protection Act.

5. Who is responsible for supervising the operation of the Data Protection Act?

   a. The Home Secretary.
   b. The Data Protection Registrar.
   c. Homeland Security.
   d. The Information Commissioner's Office.

ANSWERS

1. The correct answer is b. Copyright on sound recordings lasts for 50 years. There is no form of copyright that lasts for 25 years (a) or 100 years (d). Copyright on literary, dramatic, musical or artistic works normally lasts for 70 years (c).

2. The correct answer is c. DRM stands for Digital Rights Management. The other answers are meaningless.

3. The correct answer is a. The technique of hiding a message or a fingerprint in a graphics file is known as Steganography. Stenography (b) is another name for shorthand. Spectroscopy (c) is a method of analysing substances. Speleology (d) is the study of caves.

4. The correct answer is c. The Regulation of Investigatory Powers Act gives government agencies the right to monitor email. The Computer Misuse Act (a) makes it illegal to use a computer system without the explicit permission of the owner. The Communications Act (b) makes it illegal to obtain Internet access dishonestly. The Data Protection Act (d) gives individuals the right to know what information is held about them and tries to ensure that personal information is handled properly.

5. The correct answer is d. The Information Commissioner's Office is responsible for supervising the operation of the Data Protection Act. The Home Secretary (a) is not responsible for this area. The Data Protection Registrar used to be responsible for supervising the operation of the Data Protection Act, but this is no longer the case. Homeland Security is an American agency which has no role in the UK.

GLOSSARY

Adware: Malicious software which displays pop-up ads on a computer.

Anti-Spyware Software: Software designed to remove spyware from computers and prevent further infection.

Antivirus Software: Software designed to remove virus infection from computers and prevent further infection.

Blacklist: A list of programs prohibited from running on a computer or of email or server addresses from which email will not be accepted.

Boot Record: A small program that runs automatically when a computer is started.

Boot Sector Virus: A virus that attaches itself to the boot record of a disk.

Content Filtering: The process of allowing or blocking access to websites according to their content.

Content Rating: A system which allows web masters and content creators to label their content in categories such as nudity, sex, language, violence and other potentially harmful material.

Cyberbullying: Bullying or harassment by means of email, instant messaging, text messages, blogs, mobile phones or websites.

Digital Fingerprint: A unique label inserted into each copy of the content, eg: an e-book or an image, allowing individual copies to be identified.

Digital Rights Management (DRM): A method of controlling the number of times downloaded content can be copied and the number or types of devices it can be played on.

Digital Watermarking: A technique for protecting digital images from unauthorised use by marking them in such a way that their source can be identified.

DoS (Denial of Service) Attack: An attack with floods a server with messages, making it unavailable to normal users.

Drive-By Download: A program which is surreptitiously downloaded when a user visits a web site.

Emoticons: Combinations of keyboard character used to express a sentiment or an expression, eg: :) for smile, or :(for frown. Also known as "Smileys".

Ethical Hackers: Security experts who try to break into a computer system in order to let the owners know about security flaws. Also known as "White-Hat Hackers".

File Infector Virus: A virus which infects executable files, such as programs.

Firewall: A program which prevents hackers from accessing a computer system.

Grooming: Actions taken by an adult to form a trusting relationship with a young person, with the intention of encouraging them to take part in some kind of sexual activity.

Hackers: Malicious individuals who attempt to gain unauthorised access to a computer system, often with the intention of stealing data or causing damage.

Identity Theft: The fraudulent use of someone's personal details to open bank accounts or obtain credit cards.

Image Spam: A type of spam which displays its message as an image to avoid detection by spam filters.

Image Virus: A virus hidden within an image file, such as a photograph or drawing.

IP Address A unique address allocated to every computer on a network, normally written as four decimal numbers, separated by full stops, e.g. 192.168.23.18.

Key Logger: A program which monitors every key a user presses.

Logic Bomb: A malicious program that lies dormant until a specified trigger event occurs.

Lottery Scam: A scam in which users receive an e-mail telling them they have won a fortune in a non-existent lottery.

Macro Virus: A virus written in a scripting language, such as JavaScript, which infects application files like Word or Excel documents.

Malware: Malicious software, such as viruses, spyware and adware.

Memory-Resident Virus: A virus which lurks in memory, waiting to infect other programs

Multipartite Virus: A virus which infects both the boot record and executable files. Also known as a "Polypartite Virus".

Netiquette: A suggested set of rules for online behaviour.

Nigerian Letter: A scam in which users are asked to assist in transferring large amounts of money from an overseas country.

Packet Sniffer: A monitoring tool which can be used by network administrators or hackers to view the contents of data packets transferred over a network.

PDF Spam: A type of spam which puts its message in a PDF (Portable Data Format) file to avoid detection by spam filters.

Pharming: Redirection web traffic to a bogus website, usually with the intention of collecting confidential information.

Phishing: A technique used to persuade users to part with financial details by sending emails that are supposedly from their bank.

Polymorphic Virus: A virus which can change itself, so that antivirus software can no longer recognise it by its signature.

Polypartite Virus: A virus which infects both the boot record and executable files. Also known as a "Multipartite Virus".

Port Scanner: A monitoring tool which can be used by network administrators or hackers to find out which ports on a computer are available for use.

Proxy Server: A program which hides the true IP address of a system and replaces it with a fake one.

Ransomware: A type of malware which encrypts the data on a user's hard disk and demands money to decrypt it.

Rogue Dialler: A program which takes over a user's telephone line and makes calls to premium-rate numbers.

Rootkit: A type of malicious software which opens a backdoor to a system, allowing access to hackers.

Screensaver Virus: A virus hidden within a screensaver.

Smileys: Combinations of keyboard character used to express a sentiment or an expression, eg: :) for smile, or :(for frown. Also known as "Emoticons".

Social Engineering: A technique used to persuade users to part with confidential information by pretending to be someone they trust.

Spam: Unsolicited bulk e-mail.

Spam Filter: A program which checks a user's email for spam and rejects any suspicious messages found.

Spyware: Malicious software which can monitor a user's activities on a computer or even take partial control of the computer.

Stealth Virus: A virus that tries to hide from antivirus software

Steganography: A process used to hide identifying information or coded messages in digital images.

Time Bomb: A malicious program that lies dormant until a specified date is reached.

Trojan: A file which has malicious software hidden within it.

Virus: A malicious program which can execute on an infected computer and replicate itself.

Virus Hoax: An e-mail message claiming to warn recipients of a non-existent virus threat.

White-Hat Hackers: Security experts who try to break into a computer system in order to let the owners know about security flaws. Also known as "Ethical Hackers".

Whitelist: A list of programs permitted to run on a computer or of email or server addresses from which email will be accepted.

Worm: A malicious program that can replicate from system to system without requiring human intervention.